Crochet fo

30 Perfect Patterns to Pamper Pets

By Linda Kastiel Kozlowski

www.ComfortForCritters.org

By purchasing this book, you are supporting the Comfort for Critters program, which donates free handmade blankets to comfort homeless pets living in 400+ animal shelters across the US. While these pets await adoption, the blankets provide a comfortable bed year-round. When they are adopted, their blanket goes with them, providing something familiar as they adjust to their "forever family."

This book, as with everything I do, is dedicated to my mom.

She taught me everything useful in life,

beginning with crocheting the perfect Granny Square.

PATTERNS INSIDE

Quick reference guide to find your favorite pattern. Enjoy!!!

PUDDLES MARIA

It was one of the hardest choices I've ever made. Normally my gut will lead me in an unmistakable direction, with my conscience playing a supporting role. Decisions usually come quick, even when I'd rather delay a hard choice. But this time was different. We were adding to our family and I was staring into the eyes of Anna and Benjamin. Brother and sister, sharing a small enclosure at the DuPage County Animal Shelter. The question was, "Who would be joining me on the car ride home?"

The decision was especially difficult because this was the first time I was choosing a pet to join our family. I stood there looking at these two precious kitties, but also back at my childhood, where pets were not allowed. Well, almost not allowed. I hoped that this kitty would be spending decades with me, and I knew that we would spare nothing to give him, or her, a full and happy life. This kitty would win the lottery, but my family would certainly win too.

The first "pet" to join me as a child, was a tiny black kitten, after she was abandoned by her mother. Her hideaway, in our neighbor's camper, was discovered soon after she gave birth, and she ran for the hills. The kittens scattered as well, except for this one. I nursed her for two days, but fate had other plans for her. She passed away in my 10-year-old hands, and my heart broke. I changed that day, but my parents changed as well. It broke my father's heart to see what I went through, so pets were officially banned going forward. Looking back on the situation, and having experience now with my own pets, I realize that money played a role as well. Caring for pets properly is expensive, and with four kids, adding another mouth to feed wasn't a great idea.

That all changed when I turned 18, became an "adult", and more importantly had a boyfriend who wasn't afraid of my dad! For my 18th birthday he gave me a kitten named "Puddles Maria" and I was in love at first sight (but only with the kitten, not the guy!). That "critter" accompanied me through life for over 20 years, and was my emotional support animal before there was such a thing. She got me through college, a failed first marriage, moving to the west coast and back, and the loss of both my parents. She was there through more pregnancies than I care to count, and welcomed home both my sons into our family. She taught me that the creatures we share our home with, inhabit a section of our heart reserved only for them. It's a love that's not greater, nor lesser, than other loves. It's completely different, boasting a beauty all its own.

So as I gazed into the green eyes of the two kitties before me, I felt the weight of the decision. I then decided, Anna would be joining our family. Having a husband and two small boys at home, I thought I needed to balance the scales a bit and add another female to the mix. In case you're wondering, all our subsequent pets (and we've had many), are female!

So the decision was made by my gut, and now my conscience stepped forward to do its thing. I remember asking if there was anything, ANYTHING, I could do for all the kitties that I couldn't take home that day. I was thinking of Benjamin, but certainly couldn't look him in the eye. It was then that I felt a tap on my shoulder, from a familiar Guide, and a "calling". As the shelter worker explained that I could bring in old towels, which would be used in the cats' enclosures (giving them something soft to lay on), I knew just what I was being prompted to do. I asked if they'd accept crocheted blankets instead. With that, Comfort for Critters was born.

I learned to crochet around the time that black kitten passed away, and had kept it up by crocheting baby blankets for my boys and any baby who joined my extended family. However, crocheting went from a hobby to become my passion at that single moment. The shelter was thrilled, and a bit surprised, and even promised to send my blankets home with the pets, once they were adopted. They explained that having the scent of the shelter on the blankets would provide comfort for the pets as they adjusted to their new surroundings in their forever home. This was the first of many pieces that just fell into place for Comfort for Critters. I knew how much my two boys had loved their blankets, and how attached they became. It was truly their "comfort object" of choice. Why should a four-legged critter be any different?

So the journey began in a single shelter, with a single kitten named Anna. I thought I'd make a handful of blankets, dropping them off as I had time. As the saying goes, "if you want to make God laugh, tell Him your plans." I would soon learn about just how many shelters there are, how underfunded and understaffed they are, and just how much of a need for comfort there was in the world. Much to my surprise (and sadness), that need for comfort has only grown, over the years.

Animal Shelters

The history of animal shelters can be traced back to 1869, and a woman named Caroline Earle White. Caroline's parents made sure she received a good education, something which was highly unusual for girls at that time. She witnessed the inhumane treatment animals received in her neighborhood, and it affected her deeply. It wasn't pets who she saw mistreated, but the horses and mules who would pull heavy wagons down the streets of Philadelphia. Drivers would beat, and otherwise abuse, the animals to get them to keep going, or to move faster. Caroline never forgot these scenes, and when she married an attorney in 1854 who supported her concerns, her "animal activism" began.

She formalized this activism by joining the board of the newly created Pennsylvania Society for the Prevention of Cruelty to Animals in 1867. After being relegated to non-management roles at the PSPCA, she decided that her future would have to be with an organization where women were in charge. She, along with 29 other women, started their own branch of the PSPCA in 1869, with a focus on helping the many stray dogs in the area. This branch, called the "Women's Animal Center", became the first animal shelter in the United States, and is still open today in Bensalem, Pennsylvania.

Among the many things this first shelter, and Caroline White, accomplished was the establishment of the American Anti-Vivisection Society (in 1883), the installation of water fountains in cities so that the horses and mules had clean drinking water, the opening of the first clinic in the US which provided free veterinary care for those unable to pay, and promoting legislation in 1907 that enforced the humane treatment of animals being transported on the country's railroad system. Wow, what an amazing group of ladies! It reminds me of one of my favorite quotes by Margaret Mead, *"Never doubt that a small group of thoughtful, committed citizens can change the world; indeed, it's the only thing that ever has."*

Of course, the Women's Animal Center went on to care for cats and other animals, and promoted the concept of "sheltering animals." With their example in place, other cities followed suit. Tremendous growth happened in the 20th Century as towns identified two important roles for shelters to play, in the lives of their citizens. Shelters would provide care and protection for homeless pets, but would also protect citizens from any dangers posed by some animals. These dangers included pet bites, attacks and zoonotic diseases.

Today there are roughly five thousand animal shelters in the United States. The term "Humane Society" and "SPCA" (Society for the Prevention of Cruelty to Animals) are generic labels, which can be used by any organization. There's no affiliation with any national, or larger, group. Since it's an unstructured industry, concrete numbers on what's happening inside shelters are hard to come by. Amazingly (at least to me) there's simply no national reporting agency for animal shelters.

There are approximately 90 million dogs in the country and 94 million cats, but only about 25-30% of those pets came through the animal shelter system. Animal shelters will see 6 to 6.5 million pets come through their doors in a typical year. Of these, roughly half are cats, and the other half dogs. Sadly, only about 50% of those "critters" find forever homes.

Now is probably a good time to address the "Kill" versus "No Kill" issue, in caring for abandoned pets. The second most common question I'm asked is, "Why would Comfort for Critters help any shelter that didn't have a firm 'no-kill' policy?" (For the most common question, you'll have to read beyond this section!). I sadly know that my answer to this question is what keeps some volunteers off the CFC team.

Support Kill or No-Kill Shelters? Not such an easy question!

So exactly why would we provide our free blankets to animal shelters which are not designated as "no-kill"? Allow me to provide some good news and bad news. The good news is that pet overpopulation has fallen dramatically since the 1970s. At that time, animal control agencies euthanized up to 20 million pets every year. This common practice was done simply to control the pet population. The US Humane Society estimates that during that decade, a full 25% of the nation's dogs were simply living on the street. Another positive trend, which has helped drive down euthanasia, is the dramatic increase in households with pets. In the 1970s, there were 67 million households with pets, but today that number is 135 million!

As recently as 1990, 17 million pets were euthanized in animal shelters. While the numbers have improved, the bad news remains, that today there are roughly 2-4 million pets euthanized. One estimate for 2018, indicates only 2 million pets were euthanized. Way too many, to be sure, but a huge improvement. So how did this happen? It's another example of an issue that seems insurmountable, until someone takes it on! Or in this case, a group of committed citizens in sunny California.

About 20 years ago, the "no-kill" movement began in San Francisco, California. This community banded together and committed to finding a home for every pet that entered its shelters. Their campaign promoted adoption and used spaying and neutering as a better way to control the cat and dog population. Fortunately, this idea soon spread throughout the US, saving millions of pets each and every year.

There's also been a very active campaign for pet adoption in the last couple of decades. Rescuing a pet is now seen as the "badge of honor" that it is! Today, many families would never consider going to a pet store to add to their family. Animal shelters are the only place they would turn, which has dramatically increased adoption rates.

Great shelters are constantly trying new tactics to help with pet overpopulation. Some shelters use TNR (trap, neuter, return) to control colonies of community cats, which reside in their area. Other rescue groups will transport animals from southern states, which have a higher rate of euthanasia, to shelters in the north with high populations of potential adopters. The ASPCA reports relocating 40,000 animals, in this way, during 2018. All this results in fewer animals being killed, but the level has (unfortunately) not yet reached zero.

Many, but not all, animal shelters today are considered "no-kill". These facilities will only euthanize a pet for extreme medical necessity, when no amount of care will help the pet to lead a happy life. These facilities can euthanize up to 10% of their pets, due to temperament or health, and still be considered "no kill." These shelters range from very small to quite large, employing staff and volunteers who are among the best people on the planet. The most outstanding of these shelters, when they start receiving too many animals, will set up a system of foster-care homes to care for the overflow of pets (CFC supports these groups too!).

Though it seems like "no-kill" animal shelters should be the only shelters that win our support, it isn't always that simple. No-kill shelters are in reality "limited-admission" shelters, because they can be selective about which animals they take in. There are sometimes age limitations, behavioral requirements, and health standards which must be met, in order to surrender an animal. These requirements clearly help them limit the number of pets they will need to euthanize.

Open-admission (or "kill") shelters have no such requirements. These are typically municipal animal control agencies, who accept homeless pets from families and animal control agents. They are required to take in all animals, regardless of health, temperament or even available space. Therefore, they are sometimes forced to euthanize a pet sooner, rather than later, in order to protect the health and safety of the rest of their pet population. The shelters which are given this task are usually government run, led by people who clearly love animals and often consider this job to be their calling. Trust me, they are not doing it for the paycheck. Theirs is a tough, tough job, and one deserving of our empathy.

Having worked directly with individuals at both types of shelters, it's clear that compassion, caring and an intense love for all pets is abundant at both. It's for this reason, to support these awesome people, that CFC supports both open-admission and no-kill shelters. For me it was an easy decision and clearly in line with our mission.

Can you even make a difference?

So on to the most common question I'm asked…. "How can you even hope to make a difference, when there are millions of pets in shelters?" I do understand a person's heart when they ask me this. With so many animals going through shelters each year, it's hard to see how we'll make an impact in any meaningful way. But that's only when you look from 35,000 feet up, not from standing outside the enclosure of a homeless pet.

When I get this question, I often recite this favorite story of mine. It's sometimes told about jellyfish, sometimes starfish (my preference). When I heard it in 2007, it was yet another piece, falling perfectly into place.

~~~~~~

The Star Thrower

One day a man was walking along a beach. The sun was shining, and it was a beautiful day. Off in the distance he could see a young boy going back and forth between the surf's edge and the beach. Back and forth the boy went.

As the man approached, he could see that there were hundreds of starfish stranded on the sand as the result of the natural action of the tide. The man was struck by the apparent futility of the task. There were far too many starfish. Many of them were sure to die.

As he approached, the boy continued the task of picking up starfish one by one and throwing them back into the sea. As he came up to the boy he said, "You must be crazy! There are thousands of miles of beach covered with starfish. You can't possibly make a difference."

The boy looked at the man. He then bent down and picked up one more starfish and threw it back into the sea. He turned back to the man and said, "But it made a difference to that one."

~~~~~~

With that beautiful ending in mind, let's continue our story of comforting critters and explore all the unexpected blessings that have sprouted up. So many of these benefits were neither planned, nor anticipated by me. The credit for these goes elsewhere indeed. A huge part of the "magic" belongs to the dozens of volunteers who joined early on, and continues with the hundred or so who signed up this past year. It does "take a village", or more specifically a group of thoughtful, committed citizens, to make things happen....and happen they did!

UNEXPECTED BLESSINGS

Why blankets?

I've been fortunate enough to have been interviewed by some local, and even national, publications which wanted to shed light on our mission and provide us with some much-needed publicity. The reporter's typical first question is, "why blankets?" After I explain the hardness of the enclosures or the coldness of the floors, they think they have their answer. Boy, are they wrong!

It's then that I launch into all the blessings that the blankets bring to the shelters, pets and families. If you're making blankets, or considering supporting our mission, just check out all the ways these little bundles of fabric, yarn and fleece, really do make a difference.

Blankets boost adoption rates!

That's a big claim I know, and one that I never saw coming. However, I've heard this from too many shelters to not embrace its truth. A study in 2017, by Texas Tech University, explored how shelters can help boost their adoption rates. They found that people actually spend very little time visiting with a pet at a shelter, before they decide to adopt. The number one factor to the potential adopters is "how the pet appears", which extends beyond its appearance (though this is certainly important!). Families spend no more than 8 minutes (on average) viewing a pet.

I've heard from shelters, that the key is for the family to see the animal as a "pet" and not a "stray". They want to be able to easily picture the cat, dog or other pet, cuddling in their home. Seeing a cat, on a torn towel in a cage, cannot compare to the same kitty snuggled on a brightly colored, handcrafted blanket. As crafters, we forget that not everyone knows how to knit or crochet. So seeing our creations is impressive. Most people also have fond memories of a knit or crocheted blanket they had as a child, or of a relative who crafted these items. Just this feeling of family, handmade, warmth, etc. brings a wonderful vibe to those eight minutes.

This same study also found that people were more likely to adopt a pet, if the pet was relaxed and felt confident in approaching the person. Our blankets can be taken from the enclosure, along with the pet, giving them a sense of security. I'm sure that this helps relax them and makes for a better experience all around.

A similar study by this same university, done in 2016, showed that adoption rates rose 2.5 times, when the shelter would allow the pet to take their favorite toy, when meeting a family. These toys likely made the pet more comfortable, much as our blankets would.

As a matter of fact, the trend these days (for the lucky shelters who can afford it), is to add "luxury" features, like "roaming rooms" and ambient music to their facilities. These are added to reduce the animals' stress, and make the entire experience for families more inviting. Having beautiful blankets in the animal's enclosure, displayed in the open roaming rooms, or even wrapped around a pet as they are handed to a prospective mom, is a luxury indeed!

Blankets as transition objects!

A sad fact, known by many shelters, is that not all pets who are adopted find their "forever" family. A study completed in 2013, showed that six months after adoption, a full 10% of adopted pets where no longer in their adoptive home. Roughly 42% (of the 10%) were returned to the shelter, with the other 58% having been lost, died, or given to another family. The most critical period though, is really the first two weeks that a new pet is in the home. During this period, up to 25% of the pets who would ultimately be going somewhere else, had already been returned to the shelter.

This study encouraged shelters to keep in touch with the families, for the first few months after adoption. With US shelters already being overstressed, this may be asking too much. The study also explained that better materials should be sent home with the pet, since "behavioral problems" is a common reason pets are returned. Having information to send home, or a transitional comfort object, may help with some of these issues. Having a "security blanket" for the pet, not only adds to the pet's comfort, but it can help them transition into their new home.

Our blankets are used in the shelter for weeks, or even months. They take on the scent of the shelter, even though they are constantly washed. This is important, since a dog's nose is 100,000 times better at differentiating scents, than a human nose. Dogs have up to 300 million olfactory receptors in their noses, while we only have a measly 6 million. In addition, the area of their brain that is dedicated to their sense of smell is 40 times larger than ours. So clearly, their sense of smell is important to a pup's happiness!

There's no need to leave cats out in the cold, since they have amazing noses as well. A cat's sense of smell helps them explore their surroundings, find food, and tell whether someone is a friend or enemy! They have 200 million olfactory cells, which beats us mere humans as well. So, as they snuggle in their blanket, they learn the smells of every inch of it. Once they are adopted, the ability to relax in a blanket with these familiar scents, can really help in their adjustment.

So much research tells shelters to encourage a relaxing environment for the pets, post-adoption, in order to raise the odds that the pet will remain with the family. Our blankets are just one more tool for the shelter to use!

Blankets as comfort objects!

For anyone who has wrapped themselves in a warm blanket when tired, stressed or when simply relaxing on a cold night….a blanket as a comfort object needs no explanation. Blankets comfort the pets who may be laying on a cold floor, or a hard enclosure. Blankets add warmth, softness and even something to play with a bit.

Dogs will drag their blankets around with them, and cats have been known to knead their blankets. This is a high honor indeed, since the motion the cat is creating when kneading, is exactly what they did as a nursing kitten. A happy cat is one that loves to knead soft surfaces, repeating a comforting behavior they learned early on. Sometimes a kitty will even suckle their blanket a bit, further reinforcing that this behavior was learned while nursing.

Not every cat kneads the same way. Some will extend their claws, others will not. Some will even use all four legs to knead. Not every dog will treat their blanket the same either. Some love to plop right on it, others chew it a bit! Either way, our creations provide a comfort object to the pet, as they await their forever family.

Where the pet goes….the blanket goes!

Another benefit of our blankets, I learned directly from shelters early on. One shelter we supported asked if I could create blankets with a folded over area, or "pocket" in them. The shelter director explained that a key use for the blankets was when the pet was visiting the veterinarian, which they do quite a bit when they first arrive. Wrapping them in something familiar and safe, just calmed them right down. When they returned from the vet, after possibly having surgery, the shelter would tuck a warming disk into the blanket. The pet then got to relax and heal on a toasty, and familiar, blanket. The shelter thought a pocket would be very convenient for this use!

After speaking with other shelters, I discovered that the blankets were also being used for vet trips, taken to adoption events, and brought along when the pet visited with a potential family. The staff often saw that the pet felt safer, and more comfortable, with their "blankie".

I also heard from countless shelters that the families would be required to have a carrier, when they adopted a pet, but few families thought to bring anything soft to put inside for the car ride home. Our blankets were the perfect item to deliver comfort and security!

Blankets help the shelters!

Before I adopted Anna and got involved making blankets for other pets, I knew very little about animal shelters. The more CFC grew, and the more I got to know people in the sheltering arena, the more impressed I became. In my opinion, and with very few exceptions, these workers and volunteers are some of the best people in the world. Truly. Shelter workers go "above and beyond" as part of their daily routine. They take their work home (sometimes literally) and are consistently looking for more ways to help pets.

These folks are not paid nearly what they are worth, and do things to help pets that few of us would want to tackle on a daily basis. I'm consistently impressed with the people at the group of 300+ shelters we support. I love it when I hear directly from the shelters, just how thrilled they are when a box, or drop-off, of our blankets is received. Our blankets truly show our appreciation for what they do! I've heard many times that the staff really enjoys matching blankets to particular pets!

A common question I get, concerns the appropriate size for our blankets. I usually give a suggestion of 20" x 20", since this works for the most shelters. However, I also try to express that these shelters will find the best pet for whatever they receive. If it's a large, fleece blanket, then a larger dog may receive it. If it's smaller than even the 20" suggestion, it'll be used with a kitten. These folks are great at making the most of what they receive, and they always are appreciative!

On top of this, these shelters are consistently in need of bedding of some sort, so our blankets fill that very practical need. Of course, their effect on adoption rates, really make the shelters and workers happy as well! While I think they truly enjoy the time they get to spend with these homeless pets, their ultimate goal is to have an empty shelter, with every four-legged friend finding their family!

Blankets are treasured by the families!

A discussion on animal shelter pets is not complete without talking about the wonderful, awesome, generous, amazing families that make the choice to "adopt" and not "shop." Can you tell how much I admire these folks? As I mentioned before, a very practical use for our blankets is to make the carrier comfortable during the ride home, when a pet is adopted. I'm sure the families appreciate this bonus, but I've heard the gratitude goes beyond that.

For our volunteers who knit, crochet, make tied fleece blankets and sew, it's easy to take for granted your skills and your artistry. Yes, you all are "fiber artists!" I know in my own family, though I was raised with three sisters, I'm the only one who took up the craft. So knowing how to weave fiber into fabulousness is rare indeed....and getting rarer by the generation!

So when these families learn that they get to take home the handmade blanket that's wrapped around their pet, they are impressed indeed. They may never have made anything similar! They truly appreciate that it takes skill, time, and a whole lot of caring.

I've heard from families how thankful they are that someone cared enough about their new little family member to craft something for them. It warms their heart to know their little one was loved by someone, in addition to the wonderful care they received at the shelter.

They also appreciate that they now have a "blankie" that belongs only to their pet. Our blankets can become a cherished keepsake, kept long after the pet is gone. This aspect of our mission to "comfort" honestly never occurred to me. It wasn't until people relayed stories to me, that I realized that the comfort we provide extends beyond the pet, to the family, just when it is needed most. Wow, do I feel grateful to be able to play a small part!

COMFORT FOR CRITTERS

Why join the Comfort for Critters team?

The mission to comfort homeless pets certainly didn't start with CFC. We've just joined a large team of individuals, companies and non-profit groups that care about animals and work to make the world just a bit better for them. So there's certainly no requirement to join our team, in order to help pets!

As I've developed the group over the past dozen or so years, I've seen other organizations and people taking the blanket idea we've championed (but not invented, to be sure!) and running with it. I can't know the specific numbers, but I'd estimate (conservatively) that for every blanket donation we've made, and I track, there's probably two blankets that are created outside of our system. I base this on the dozens of emails I get every day requesting patterns, shelter information, etc. from people who are not on our list of volunteers. I am eager to help them and think it's simply wonderful that they are taking up the baton and helping shelter pets independently. Comforting pets is the ultimate goal and I don't care one bit how it gets done or especially who gets credit!

With that said, I do think there are some advantages to working within the CFC system, and I hope the structure makes it easy to help and rewarding to the individuals. I know not everyone has enough extra money to buy all the yarn they will be using (I know I don't!), so I try to be a clearinghouse for free yarn to anyone local. I know not every shelter has time to send thank you notes, so I try to email, or mail, a thank you to everyone, for whatever they've done to help. I know not everyone has time to make sure a shelter will use their blankets, or that they even need blankets, so I try to provide a constantly updated list of shelters and include any specific requirements I hear from the shelters.

I think the biggest reason for going through our system is that you can be assured of how your blankets will be used. I have stacks of emails from people who donated blankets independently, only to find out the shelter didn't need blankets, would not use "yarn" blankets, or wasn't sending them home with the pets when they were adopted. Our system is not perfect, but every shelter on our list has: 1) expressed a need for blankets, 2) told me that they have no problem with giving knit or crocheted blanket to their pets (there are a few exceptions, which are called out on our website list) and 3) they have committed to sending the blanket home with the pet when they are adopted. Some shelters were already doing something similar with a towel or toy, to other shelters it was a brand-new idea, which they loved!

So besides making it super-easy to find a shelter near you (or at least in your state) who wants your blankets, I truly hope CFC is always a blessing in the lives of the volunteers. I don't say this lightly. I really want the volunteers to feel great about what they're doing, and why they are doing it. I want every supporter to embrace the change they will bring to their corner of the world. There are tons of more practical benefits as well...

Crafting blankets is the perfect way to use up any leftover yarn you may have from a project. As most crafters would agree, it's nearly impossible to toss our extra supplies! CFC let's you put them to use! The blankets are easy to make, since any method and any stitch will work.

Speaking of stitches, it's also a great way to try out a new technique or new stitch, without having to commit to an entire project. I've learned the hard way, while making afghans for my family, that sometimes a stitch which is quirky-but-fun at first, quickly become tedious. Argh...only 6 more feet to go!

Our little blankets are the perfect place to try out a new stitch, experiment, blend weird colors, etc. It should be a creative outlet, where there truly are no mistakes. If there is the occasional slipped stitch, it certainly won't be pointed out by the lucky cat, dog or ferret who receives the blanket!

Whenever people ask me if they can make blankets a new, creative way, my answer is a consistent "yes!" As long as it's washable, it's usable! Be creative, have fun, express yourself as only you can! Like they say, "be yourself….no one can tell you you're doing it wrong!"

More surprises…

When I started CFC, my goal was to bless all the little lives, which I could not adopt. I soon found out that blessings have a way of multiplying. They fall in unexpected ways and in unexpected areas. These are just a handful of the ways people have told me that making these little blankets has blessed their life. I could not be more grateful for this feedback!

- Crafting blankets helps people stop smoking! When the urge strikes to light up (after dinner?) they pick up the crochet hook or knitting needles instead.
- For people with traumatic brain injuries, making a blanket is truly therapeutic. Both the repetitive nature of the stitches and the fine motor skill development, can really help in their long process of healing.
- Making blankets helps with weight loss or weight maintenance. It's hard to snack in front of the television, when you're knitting or crocheting!
- Making blankets has give some retired folks a new "job" to use their skills and expertise.

- Volunteering in such a fun manner is a great way to fulfill community service hours or add "volunteering" to a resume.

- For people who can't leave their home to volunteer, due to family obligations, it gives them an opportunity to help others.

- For crafters who have run out of people who would like a handmade scarf or afghan, they now have a whole country full of pets who would love their creations.

- For individuals with anxiety and depressive disorders, venturing out to volunteer can be difficult. Making blankets gives them the opportunity to give back and see how they are contributing to others in a meaningful way.

- Making tied-fleece blankets for cute kittens and puppies are the perfect way to introduce kids to volunteering. Children as young as five, on up to college age, have really enjoyed helping pets by making tied-fleece blankets.

It was probably discovering the effect on the volunteers, more than anything else, that has kept me going all these years. I hope this list just grows and grows as we continue with our mission. To help, I've tried to line up as many helpful tools as possible. If you're not taking advantage of these yet, please do!

Website

The website remains the greatest resource for volunteers. Any new tool which I create, will find a home somewhere on the site. Here's what else you'll find online:

- Monthly newsletter so you can track our progress towards comforting pets and see what we've accomplished together each month.
- Inspirational pictures of shelter pets on our blankets.
- Lots of thank you notes, from grateful shelters, showing our blankets in use!
- Full list of all participating shelters, along with contact names and any special requests from the shelter. This list is updated every week, if not every day!
- Volunteer information packet, to learn what we're all about.
- Free patterns for knit, crochet and fleece blankets, along with other crafting information and tips.
- Interesting articles on pets, crafting and volunteering topics!
- Donation forms you can use when shipping, or dropping off, blankets to a shelter on our list.
- Helpful guidelines for groups which may want to help shelter pets as a project.

Social Media

You'll find Comfort for Critters on all major social media, including Facebook, Instagram and Pinterest. We post interesting articles, lots of humor and fun pictures. We try to be an island of positivity!

Groups

In 2019, CFC began to move towards getting volunteers to interact directly with each other. To accomplish this, we launched our first Meetup group in Lisle,

Illinois (near our home-base in Glen Ellyn). Local volunteers get together monthly at the main library, to share yarn, snacks and laughs. It's been a lot of fun!

For volunteers outside of our immediate area, we launched "The Comfort for Critters Team" as a private group on Facebook. It's a group where everyone is welcomed and appreciated, and (most of all) it's 100% positive! We encourage members to post the blankets they're working on, funny memes and pictures of their pets. It's a great place to ask a question and get encouragement too. We also share patterns and tips on local yarn sales!

Shelter list

The shelter list is really the heart and soul of CFC. It's a long list of over 300 US shelters (and a handful of Canadian ones), but we obviously live in a very big country! So while every state, has at least a couple of shelters, there may not be a shelter close enough for you to drop off your blankets. If this is the case, please contact me via the website and I'll try to sign up a shelter near you. It almost always works out, and I'm happy to do it!

On the other hand, if you drop off blankets at a shelter and have a bad experience (for whatever reason), please reach out to me and let me know. This does happen from time to time. I will reach out to my contact at the shelter, and do my best to resolve the situation or at least give you more information on your concern. Occasionally we do need to remove a shelter from our list, since I always want our creations going to the best shelters, who will appreciate them every time. The volunteers are my eyes and ears, so please report back to me if you feel it's necessary.

Materials

From the materials that are donated to me (I never spend our funds on buying yarn or fleece), I provide free yarn and fleece to all local volunteers (or anyone who stops by my home in Glen Ellyn, IL). I don't always have fleece, but I do always stay stocked up on yarn. It's available 24/7 via a bench outside my front door. So stop by if you're in the neighborhood (email me for the address)!

For those who can't make it to Glen Ellyn, the website has ready-made posts for volunteers to use on their social media accounts to receive yarn and fleece donations directly. There's also a flyer you can post at your local fabric or craft store, which promotes what we do and can be used to request material donations.

Free Blanket Distribution

Since we started in Illinois, the majority of our volunteers are in the Chicagoland area. All the blankets dropped off at CFC headquarters in Glen Ellyn, Illinois are shipped (at no cost to the volunteer), to 300+ shelters across the US. We're donating over 1,500 blankets regularly every single month! To pay this shipping cost, and our other business expenses, we now sell t-shirts (for pet and craft lovers), some blankets (only ones made by me), and this e-book. So THANK YOU for helping to keep our mission going!

More resources coming!

When I started CFC, I would crochet my blankets at every soccer, baseball or basketball practice, or game, I attended. Having two boys in year-round sports, helped me comfort many pets! This also helped launch the group, since people were always asking me what I was doing. They graciously began donating yarn and asking enough questions, that I realized a website was necessary. That's how

CFC "grew up" over the years...someone asking for a resource and me trying my best to put that together to benefit everyone.

So....if you find there's something missing, and it would help you participate, please email me at Linda@comfortforcritters.org. I work on new "tools" each and every month. It's hard to predict what's coming next, mainly because no one has asked for it yet. I can't promise to fulfill every wish, but once again, I'll do my best!

PERFECT PATTERNS

Perfect Patterns to Pamper Pets

Now comes the real "heart" of this book! I just love trying new stitches, combining colors and being creative with my blankets. I know many of our volunteers do as well. These patterns have all been assembled by me, as I found interesting stitches, sometimes tweaked them a bit, and then created a blanket perfectly sized for most pets. Keep in mind, that if you crochet tighter or looser, that will alter the final size. Remember though, the shelters help pets in all sorts of sizes, so if your blanket is a little bigger (or a lot) that's perfect too! Even smaller creations will be used by guinea pigs, kittens and other small pets.

Also keep in mind, as you try these new stitches and techniques, that we don't need to strive for perfection. Our blankets are better than perfect, they're handmade! Winston Churchill said, "Perfection is the enemy of progress" and I think he must have been thinking about pet blankets when he said that. Let your goal be to make progress on a stitch, or a blanket, or a technique. Assure yourself, that the shelter and pet will appreciate whatever you create with love.

Speaking of imperfection.... I tried very hard to double check all the patterns, making two of each blanket. However, I too am human! So if you see a mistake, please email me a correction (info@comfortforcritters.org). Please try to be as specific as possible. I will sincerely appreciate it and will make the change in the book asap!

As you read though the patterns, please notice that I've laid out each pattern so you can simply print out that page and you're ready to create. Every page has a key, pictures of the finished blanket I made, and a few surprises. For starters, you'll see pictures of pets enjoying handmade blankets. Every single picture is from a shelter we support, showing CFC blankets in use! You'll also find quotes from the thank you notes I've received from shelters, and comments I've gotten from CFC volunteers.

Sometimes when the days get long, the funds grow short and I'm just too tired to crochet one more blanket, I flip through my "smile file". I started it shortly after I began CFC. It contains letters, messages, cards and tokens of appreciation that inspire me. It's "magic" is that it always returns me to my purpose and puts a smile on my face. I hope these pictures and quotes can be your smile file, for when I've made a mistake in a pattern or it's just been "one of those days"!

Blanket in the Round

I don't quite know why, but I'm just drawn to making these round and colorful blankets. Part of the allure is that I get to use up the tiny bits of leftover yarn, which I don't bag for volunteers (they are way too small). I just love keeping them out of the landfill and crafting them into super-colorful blankets! I sometimes use only solid colors (pictured on the left), and other times I alternate a row of solid with a row of variegated yarn (pictured on the right). It truly all depends on what I have in front of me at the time! Either way, they always turn out beautifully.

Special Note from Linda: If the blanket begins to "ripple" (rather than laying flat) after any of the rows, just do one complete row of all DC all the way around (ie. do not put 2 DC in any one space). This helps the blanket lay flat. It's a bit of trial and error, to get a round blanket to lay flat, but stick with it! With that said, please don't be concerned if it still does "ripple" a bit. The pets will love curling up on it just the same (maybe even more so)!

Gather your comfort tools: Use a crochet hook size "I" and one skein washable yarn. As I mentioned, it's a great way to use the little bits of extra yarn you may have. Even a very small ball of yarn will finish one row around. Have fun switching colors and being creative!

Get started helping pets - CH 5, SL to join into a ring.

Row 1 - CH 2 (counts as DC), 11 DC into the center of the ring, SL to join, tie off. *At start of each row you'll join a new color (if you want) into the top of any space that has 2 DC. I find that I can just "stitch over" the tail of the previous color, so that I don't have to "weave in" the end!*

Row 2 – CH 2, DC in the same ST as the CH 2, 2 DC in all ST from previous row, sl to join (24 total dc, counting CH 2 at start), tie off.

Row 3 - CH 2, DC in same ST as the CH 2, DC in next ST,*2 DC, 1 DC*, repeat between * around the circle, SL to join, tie off.

Row 4 - CH 2, DC in same ST as the CH 2, DC into the next 2 ST, *2DC, 1 DC in next 2 ST*, repeat between * around the circle, SL to join, tie off.

Row 5 - CH 2, DC in same ST as the CH 2, DC into the next 3 ST, *2 DC, 1 DC in next 3 ST*, repeat between * around the circle, SL to join, tie off.

Row 6 - CH 2, DC in same ST as the CH 2, DC into the next 4 ST, *2 DC, 1 DC in next 4 ST*, repeat between * around the circle, SL to join, tie off.

Row 7 - 16 - Continue with additional rows, following the same pattern as above, until blanket is the desired size. Each additional row will have one more dc between sets of 2 dc in one space.

Key: CH – chain
SL - slip stitch
ST – stitch
HDC - half double crochet
DC - double crochet

Lemon Peels Delight

I love making this blanket, especially for shelter pets. It has a wonderful texture, which is just perfect for kitties to knead! With two strands of yarn it's also a fairly "tight" stitch, which is great as well for the shelters. I like using two strands (whenever possible) so that I can create blankets with unusual color combinations. Two strands will make the blanket thick, unique and colorful … while also using whatever leftover yarn you have!

Gather your comfort tools: I suggest using two different colors of 4-ply yarn and a "K" sized crochet hook for best results. However, thicker yarn and a larger hook would work too.

Get started helping pets - CH 32 (you can do more chains or less, just make sure it's an even number).

Row 1 – Work SC into second chain from hook, then DC, then SC (alternate DC and SC across to the end).

Row 2- Chain 1, start with SC (you should be going into a DC in the row below), then DC, using alternating pattern across to the end. Just be sure to put a SC into the top of the DC from the previous row, and a DC into the top of a SC from the previous row.

Row 3+ - Create as many rows as needed, to make a square blanket. If you started with an even number of chains, each row should start the same as row 2.

Matching Border - Do not fasten off. Turn, CH1, SC in 1st ST, SC in each ST around using 3 SCs in each corner, SL in first SC, fasten off & weave in ends.

Contrasting Border: Finish off after reaching desired length. Attach 2 strands of new color yarn, SC in 1st ST, SC in each ST around using 3 SCs in each corner, SL in beginning SC, fasten off & weave in ends.

Key:

CH – Chain

SC – Single crochet

SL – Slip stitch

ST - Stitch

DC – Double crochet

HDC – Half double crochet

What shelters have to say: "Thank you so much for the hand-made blankets! We are overwhelmed by your generosity!! The animals here at Stray Rescue will love them. Thank you again!!"   ~ Stray Rescue of St. Louis in St. Louis, MO

Poppy Crossover

This is another favorite pattern of mine, since it makes blankets with a bit of texture. Are you catching onto the theme? I love to picture the shelter pets really nestled into the blankets. So I tend to favor patterns that don't result in a "flat" blanket, but one with many lumps and bumps. However, really any blanket created with love will protect the pet from the cold floor of the enclosure. So any blanket is a comforting blanket!

Gather your comfort tools - I suggest using 2 strands of 4-ply yarn and an "N" sized hook for best results.

Get started helping pets - CH 44.

Row 1 – 2 DC in 4th CH from hook, *skip next CH, 2 DC in next CH. Repeat from * to last two CH, skip next CH, 1 DC into last CH.

Row 2 - 6 – CH3, * 2 DC in the space between 2 DC group, repeat from * across to end, put 1 DC into top of last CH3.

Row 7 & 8 – Join new color *(for row 7 only)*, CH 2, HDC in each stitch across to the end.

Row 9 - Join original color, 2 DC in 4th CH from hook, *skip next CH, 2 DC in next CH. Repeat from * to last two CH, skip next CH, 1 DC into last CH.

Row 10 - 14 - CH3, *skip next CH, 2 DC in the space between 2 DC group, repeat from * across to end, put 1 DC into top of last CH3.

Row 15 & 16 – Repeat rows 7 & 8.

Row 17 – 22 – Repeat rows 9 – 14.

Edging – This blanket ended up being a great size at 20" x 22", so I just put a SC all around the perimeter, putting 3 SC into each corner.

Key:
CH – Chain
DC – Double crochet
HDC – Half double crochet

Don't ever question the value of volunteers. Noah's Ark was built by volunteers; the Titanic was built by professionals.
~ Dave Gynn

Why volunteers help: "We cannot take in any additional pets, but I wanted to still help others find a home. Making the blankets gave me a way to help while using my crafting skills. I think the blankets will make the animals more appealing to adopters and they'll comfort the animals, making them calmer! This was my first time donating blankets and when we came to the shelter, I wasn't sure of the reception I would receive. When the ladies saw them they were so excited that I felt like my time and effort was well worth it!" *~ Catherine J. in Mays Landing, NJ*

Puff-Puff!

Get ready to make a "puffy" pet blanket with this pattern. It's almost like a miniature pillow-top mattress! I appreciated learning this stitch because it's quite large, even when using just one strand of yarn. So the blanket is created quickly and sent off to the shelter sooner, rather than later. I find I make more of these "puffy" blankets during the cold Chicago winter, wanting every shelter pet to feel the "puffs" of softness and warmth!

Gather your comfort tools - Crochet hook size "K", one skein of washable yarn and one partial skein to add a contrasting border (if you want).

Get started helping pets - CH 55, depending on the thickness of the yarn and your stitch gauge. Chain should measure approximately 20" from start to hook.

Row 1 – SC in second CH from hook * CH1, skip next CH, SC in next CH, repeat from * across to end.

Row 2 – CH2, turn, create a PUFF stitch in next CH1 space, (PUFF stitch: YO, insert hook in CH1 space and pull up a loop even with the hook. Repeat this 3 times. YO and draw through all 7 loops on the hook. CH1 to close), * CH1, work PUFF stitch in next CH1 space, repeat from * across to end, except work HDC in last SC.

Row 3 – CH1, turn, SC in first CH-1 space, CH1, * SC in next CH-1 space (between PUFFS), CH1, repeat from * across, SC in top of beginning CH.

Rows 4+ - Repeat rows 2 and 3 until piece is approximately square. Do one final row of SC across to balance the piece.

Border – Work a HDC along the perimeter of the piece using the same color yarn. Put 3 HDC into each corner to give it a nice square shape. I then added two more rows of HDC, in a contrasting color this time, but again, putting 3 HDC into each corner to keep it square.

Key:

CH – chain

SC – single crochet

YO – yarn over

HDC - half double crochet

PUFF – puff stitch (YO, insert hook in CH1 space and pull up a loop even with the hook. Repeat this 3 times. YO and draw through all 7 loops on the hook. CH1 to close.)

What shelters have to say: "*The Prattville Autauga Humane Society is SO thankful for your recent gift of homemade blankets. They are just beautiful. I posted a photo of them on our shelter Facebook page and a link to your group and it has inspired such a response! Local women can't wait to put their talents and knitting needles to use!!*"
~ Prattville Autauga Humane Society in Prattville, AL

Ribbed for Comfort

This is an interesting pattern, because it creates one smooth side and one side lined with ridges. I found it quick to work up and fun to create. I did find the "sides" (actually the end of the rows) curled up a bit as I was working. To fix this, I added an extra wide border to hold the edges down. The overall shape wasn't perfect either, but I don't strive for perfect, I strive for comfort. In my opinion, machines create "perfect"....people create imperfectly, but with love. I'd opt for "people" every single time. I hope you agree!

Special note from Linda: Creating stitches that swung around the "front post" and "back post" of previous stitches was new to me, and a bit cumbersome at first. I did figure it out eventually. I'm glad I did, since I found many other interesting stitches that used this same technique. So if you struggle with it as well, hang in there and stick with it!

Gather your comfort tools - Use 4-ply yarn and a "K" sized hook for best results.

Get started helping pets - CH 54.

Row 1 – DC in fourth CH from hook and in each CH across to the end.

Row 2 – CH 1, turn, work FPDC around the post of each ST across.

Row 3 – CH 1, turn, work BPDC around the post of each ST across.

Row 4+ – Repeat rows 2 and 3 until you reach your desired size. 20"x 20" is ideal for many pets!

Border – Since the ends of each row started curling up a bit, I added a thicker than usual border. The sample pictured has made with two rows of HDCs (3 HDC in each corner) in a contrasting color and then one row of SC (3 SC in each corner) in the first color.

Key:
CH – chain

ST – stitch

SC – single crochet

DC – double crochet

HDC – half double crochet

FPDC – front post double crochet (YO, insert hook all the way around the POST of next ST, going from FRONT to BACK, YO, pull up a loop, YO, draw through 2 loops, YO, draw through remaining 2 loops).

BPDC – back post double crochet (YO, insert hook all the way around the POST of next ST, going from BACK to FRONT, YO, pull up a loop, YO, draw through 2 loops, YO, draw through remaining 2 loops).

Why volunteers help: "I make blankets because I love all animals. We lost our dog a year ago and since both of us are near 80, we feel we're too old to adopt another. So this is my way of giving back. These homeless animals need a little TLC and much comfort before being adopted to their forever home." ~ Gavle K. in Edinbura. TX

Leanne's Weave

If you're a bit tired, after a long day, this is the stitch for you! It's a simple pattern and simple stitch (I like simple!), but it makes a truly wonderful blanket. It's easy, thick and puffy. What's not to love? As you speed through it, you'll be picturing all the pets who will enjoy your creation. That's what I did! It was suggested by one of our volunteers, Leanne T., which is always appreciated. I liked her pattern, but wanted the blanket to be super-thick, so I used two strands of yarn. This isn't 100% necessary, but I encourage you to give it a try!

Gather your comfort tools - If you're using two strands use a crochet hook size "N". Use a smaller hook ("K") if you plan to use just one strand.

Get started helping pets – CH 45.

Row 1 - DC in third CH from hook, and in each CH across to the end.

Row 2 – CH 1, turn, * SC in first ST, DC in next ST, repeat from * across to the end. Just be sure your last ST is a DC.

Row 3 - 26 – CH 1, turn, * SC **AND** DC into DC, skip next SC, repeat from * across to the last ST, put a DC into the final ST (in every other row).

Final Row (27) – For final row, repeat row 2. For the blanket pictured I needed to do 27 rows total.

Border – In a wacky move for this blanket, I used all three colors of yarn, putting a row of HDC along the perimeter, and 3 HDC into each border. It was a bit tricky to wrangle that much yarn, but I think it really tied all the colors together.

Key:

HDC - half double crochet

SC – single crochet

Why volunteers help: "*I lost two cats a week before Christmas within two days of each other. Heartbroken and depressed I want to honor them by helping this cause. I'm feeling better! I think the blankets will comfort pets in many ways. It's something of their own, made through love and energy, that will follow them to their new home. This cause has given me hope and a purpose ... it has helped me find my balance again and work through my grief. Thank you.*"   *~ Diana C. in Aurora, IL*

Be the person your dog thinks you are!

Seashells by the Seashore

I LOVE this stitch because it makes a gorgeous blanket! It looks complicated (at least to me), but it's truly easy to do. It also reminded me of the many (human) baby blankets I've made. I couldn't help but picture a kitten or puppy in a blanket made with these "seashells". It works up fast too!

I suggest using two different colors, to really show off the stitch, but this isn't necessary. In the sample above you can see how it looks if two colors are used, or just one. Enjoy!

Gather your comfort tools - I suggest using 4-ply yarn and a "K" sized hook for best results.

Get started helping pets – CH 52. *You'll be working with multiples of 6, plus 2.*

Row 1 – SC in second CH from hook, * skip next 2 CH, 5 DC in next CH, skip next 2 CH, SC in next CH, repeat from * across to end, turn.

Row 2 – CH 3 (counts as first DC), 2 DC in same stitch, skip next 2 stitches, SC in next stitch, * skip next 2 stitches, 5 DC in next stitch, skip next 2 stitches, SC in next stitch, repeat from * across until you reach the last 3 stitches, skip next 2 stitches and 3 DC into the last stitch, turn.

Row 3 – CH 1, SC in first stitch, skip next 2 DC, 5 DC in next SC, skip next 2 stitches, * SC in next stitch, skip next 2 stitches, 5 DC in next SC, skip next 2 stitches, repeat from *across to end, except put a SC in the top of the turning CH at the very end.

Row 4+ – Repeat rows 2 and 3 until you reach the desired blanket size. Be sure to end the pattern with row 3!

Final Row – CH 3 (counts as first DC), DC in same beginning stitch, skip next stitch, HDC in next stitch, SC in next stitch, * HDC in next stitch, skip next stitch, 3 DC in next stitch, skip next stitch, HDC in next stitch, SC in next stitch, repeat from * across to the end, except in the last 3 stitches, put a HDC in first stitch, skip next stitch, put 2 DC in last stitch.

Border – I wanted a finished size of roughly 18" x 22", which is a great size for many pets. The blanket ended up a bit less than that, so I made it up with a thicker than normal border. I added a row of SC all around (except 3 SC in each corner), then a row of HDC (3 in each corner) and added another row of SC (again, 3 into each corner!).

Key:
CH – chain
DC – double crochet
HDC – half double crochet
SC – single crochet

> *What shelters have to say:* "*What a great surprise to open up your box! Thank you so much. We had a ring worm outbreak and had to throw away everything. The blankets came at a great time. Thank you again! Your gift will allow us to rescue animals so that they can live a long and happy life in a loving forever home.*" *~ Little Victories Animal Rescue in Ona, WV*

It's not what we have in life, but who we have in our lives that matters.

Waves all the Way!

This is another stitch that creates a nice "bumpy" blanket. When I made the sample shown above, my own kitties, couldn't help but knead it. They don't do this for every blanket, so I took that as a good sign! I found it easy and quick to create the perfect sized pet blanket too. This would also be a good stitch if you plan to make a larger, puppy-size blanket. Just increase the initial chains!

Gather your comfort tools - I suggest using 4-ply yarn and a "K" sized hook for best results, but thicker yarn and a larger hook would work too.

Get started helping pets – CH47 to make a final blanket that will measure approximately 18" x 20".

Row 1 – SS in 3rd chain from hook (creates first HDC), * HDC in next CH, SS in next CH, * repeat from * across to the end.

Row 2 – CH 2 (counts as 1st HDC), skip first SS, * SS into next HDC, HDC in next SS, *repeat from * all the way to the end. Be sure to put a SS into the top of the ending CH2.

Row 3+ – Repeat row 2, until you reach the desired size. I ended up doing 56 rows. You can switch colors whenever you'd like, or making a solid colored blanket with a contrasting trim. Just be creative!

Border – Since this stitch shows up as little "waves" on the blanket, I opted for a plain border. I added a final row of HDC all the way across (once I reached the desired blanket size) and then continued these HDCs all around the perimeter, putting three HDCs into each corner. Since I used two colors in this blanket, I did a second row of HDCs in the other color along the perimeter, putting three HDCs in each corner.

Key:
CH – chain
SS – slip stitch
HDC - half double crochet

Why volunteers help: "All of my pets have been rescues. I have a great passion for their plight. I love to crochet but need a purpose. This is my opportunity to give back. Win, win! I hope these blankets will bring the pets a sense of safety and love. Thank you for giving me this opportunity to give of myself in a way that is so rewarding to me."
~ *Debby K. in Ambler, PA*

Striped Granny

I adore Granny Squares, since they represent what got me hooked on crochet, as a little girl. I simply love the uniformity and the combination of colors. So I was thrilled to learn a way to do the same stitch, but in rows. It just adds a bit of variety, when I want to use up bits and pieces of yarn. Hope you enjoy it as well!

Gather your comfort tools - For best results, use a 4-ply yarn and a "K" sized hook. If you decide to make your blanket a bit smaller or larger than the one this pattern creates, just be sure that your initial chain is a multiple of 3, plus 2.

Get started helping pets - CH 50.

Row 1 - Work 1 SC in 2nd CH from hook. Continue working SC into each chain till the end (turn).

Row 2 - Chain 2, then work 1 DC into first ST. *Skip 2 ST, work 3 DC all into next ST (makes a cluster) *. Repeat between * until you have just 3 ST left, skip 2 ST, then put a single DC into last ST. You will end up with a row that begins and ends with a DC, and has the "clusters" in between. *(Change yarn color, if you like!)*

Row 3 - From now on you'll be working in the spaces between the clusters of the previous row. CH 2, then work 3DC into each space between clusters. You'll end the row with a single DC into the top of the final ST in the previous row. *(Change yarn color, if you like!)*

Row 4+ - Repeat rows 2 and 3 until you reach the desired size. You can change yarn every row, or every group of rows. Just be sure to weave in all the ends (arg!).

Border – A simple border is very nice for this stitch. For the example, I trimmed the entire piece in two rows of HDC, putting 3 HDC into each corner.

Key:
CH – chain
DC – double crochet
ST - stitch
SC – single crochet
HDC – half double crochet

Why volunteers help: "Over the years, we've adopted several four-legged family members from shelters and acquired a few others from re-homing situations. Words cannot express the joy that they have brought us over the years, so this is just a small way to show our gratitude for their love and companionship. Every animal should have basic comfort, including a warm place to rest. I hope my blankets will bring a small measure of comfort and love to animals waiting to find their forever homes." *~ Elizabeth R. in Urbana, IL*

Granny in the Round

This pattern combines my love of the Granny Square, with my love of round blankets. So this pattern is just heaven to me! I also appreciate that the resulting blanket is similar to a colorful Mandala! To me it's perfect to show off a jet-black shelter pet, or really any pet. Adding color to the enclosures can brighten up the entire shelter! This is a fun blanket to make if you have lots of leftovers, but in small amounts each. Sometimes I gather all my remnants in a particular color family (blues/greens) and other times I mix and match whatever I have on hand. The result is always gorgeous. They're fast to make too!

Gather your comfort tools - I suggest using 4-ply yarn and a "K" sized hook for best results. Grab whatever leftover yarn you have and put it to good use!

Get started helping pets - CH 4 and join with SL to form a ring.

Row 1 – CH 3 (counts as DC), put 11 DC into ring, join with SL to first CH 3. (Start a new color for every row, by simply joining the yarn in any SP <u>after</u> a SGC!)

Row 2 – CH 3, DC into same SP, put 2 DC into next SP and into each SP around to the end. Join with SL to top of CH 3 from beginning.

Row 3 – CH 3, work 2 DC into same space, SGC into next SP and in every SP around to end. Join to beginning CH 3 with a SL.

Row 4 – CH 3, work 3 DC into same space, * SGC into next SP, LGC into next SP, repeat from * around to end. Join to beginning CH 3 with a SL.

Row 5 – CH 3, work 2 DC into same space, * LGC into SP in the middle of the previous rows LGC, then SGC in the next 2 SP, repeat from * around to the end, putting a LGC in the middle of the final LGC, a SGC in the last SP, and joining it with a SL to the top of the initial CH 3.

Row 6 – Repeat row 4.

Row 7 – Repeat row 3.

Row 8 – CH 3, work 3 DC into same space, * work SGC into next 2 SP, work LGC into next space, repeat from * around to end. Join to beginning CH 3 with a SL.

Row 9 – CH 3, 2 DC into same space, work a SGC into every SP and into every middle of the LGC around to end.

Row 10 – CH 3, work 3 DC into same space, * work SGC into next 3 SP, work LGC into next space, repeat from * around to end. Join to beginning CH 3 with a SL.

Row 11 – CH 3, 2 DC into same space, work a SGC into every SP and into every middle of the LGC around to end.

Row 12 – CH 3, work 3 DC into same space, * work SGC into next 4 SP, work LGC into next space, repeat from * around to end. Join to beginning CH 3 with a SL.

Row 13 – CH 3, 2 DC into same space, work a SGC into every SP and into every middle of the LGC around to end.

Row 14 – CH 3, work 3 DC into same space, * work SGC into next 5 SP, work LGC into next space, repeat from * around to end. Join to beginning CH 3 with a SL. Your blanket should now be a great size for a pet at around 21" across.

Border – You almost don't need a border for this pattern, but I always like to add a touch of black to frame the piece. I added a simple SC in SP all around the perimeter.

Key:
CH – chain
SGC – small granny cluster (3 DC into same space)
DC – double crochet

LGC – large granny cluster (4 DC into same space)

SC – single crochet

SL – slip stitch

SP – space

HDC – half double crochet

Basket Weave Fun

This pattern makes a blanket that is super snuggly. It's thicker than most other patterns, even though it uses just one strand of yarn. It's quick to work up too, once you get the hang of working around the posts. This took me a little while to get used to, but hang in there. If I figured it out, you can too!

Since we often use leftover yarn to make our pet blankets, I thought I'd make this one using a partial skein. When I ran out (about halfway through) I switched to another, contrasting color and then created a border that flip-flopped the colors. I really like the unique results. Be sure to experiment with your blankets too!

Gather your comfort tools - I suggest using 4-ply worsted weight yarn and a "K" sized hook for best results, but thicker yarn and a larger hook would work too.

Get started helping pets - CH 53.

Row 1 – DC in fourth CH from hook and in each chain across to the end. You should have 51 stitches, and it should measure about 18 inches. (Adjust, if needed, by adding multiples of 6 to the initial chain.)

Row 2 + 3 – CH 2, turn, skip the first DC, * work a FPDC (see note at bottom) around the POST of the next 3 DCs, work BPDC (see note at bottom) around the POST of the next 3 DCs. Repeat from * to the end of the row. Put a DC in the top of the last stitch.

Row 4 + 5 – CH 2, turn, skip the first DC, * work a BPDC around the POST of the next 3 DCs, work FPDC around the POST of the next 3 DCs. Repeat from * to the end of the row. Put a DC in the top of the last stitch.

Rows 6+ – Repeat rows 2 through 5, until piece is roughly square.

Border – Any type of border can be applied to this piece, from a simple SC to something more elaborate. To duplicate the blanket pictured, simply SC in each stitch along the perimeter, putting three SCs in each corner. I then went back *around with a HDC, in the same manner.*

Note from Linda:
How to create a Front Post Double Crochet (FPDC)
YO, insert hook around the post by inserting it into the hole before the stitch and then back up through the hole after the stitch (the hook should now be behind the stitch or "post"). YO and draw up a loop, YO and pull through first 2 loops on hook, YO and pull through the remaining 2 loops. You'll notice this is just like doing a DC, you're just working the hook around the post and not into the top of a stitch. The resulting FPDC should appear at the front.

How to create a Back Post Double Crochet (BPDC)
YO, insert hook around the post by inserting it <u>from the back</u> into the hole before the stitch and then back out through the hole after the stitch (the hook should now be in front the stitch or "post"). YO and draw up a loop, YO and pull through first 2 loops on hook, YO and pull through the remaining 2 loops. The resulting BPDC should appear at the back.

Key:
YO – Yarn over
BPDC – Back post double crochet
CH – Chain
DC – Double crochet
FPDC – Front post double crochet

What shelters have to say: "What a beautiful and useful donation your group sent to the pets in the care of our little shelter. Your blankets are loved by all the animals. It's like they feel the love that went into them!

Our lobby cat, Belinda, chose her favorite as we unpacked the box and she has hardly left it since! Thank you for what you do to comfort critters all over the United States, especially this little shelter in rural West Virginia!"
~ Jackson County Animal Shelter in Cottageville, WV

Teardrops of Joy

I've tried quite a few "puff" stitches over my many years learning the art of crochet (yes, I consider it an "art"!). I love how puffy they make a pet blanket, and I thought this stitch would be similar. It's not, but I like it all the same! The stitch turns out large, but it lies perfectly flat. I personally found it a lot easier to manage on the hook, than a typical puff stitch. Give it a try and see how you think it stacks up to other puffy stitches!

Gather your comfort tools - I suggest using 4-ply yarn and a "K" sized hook for best results.

Get started helping pets - CH 52.

Row 1 – SC in second CH from hook, * CH 1, skip next CH, SC in next CH, repeat from * across to end.

Row 2 – CH 3, work "teardrop" in next CH 1 space (teardrop= YO, insert hook into CH 1 space and pull up a loop, YO and draw through 2 loops on hook. Do this three times, then YO and draw through all 4 loops on hook to create a "teardrop"). * CH 1, work "group" in next CH 1 space, repeat from * across to the end, DC in last SC.

Row 3 – CH 1, * SC in next CH 1 space (between the "groups"), CH 1, repeat from * across to the end, putting a final SC into the top of the last CH.

Row 4 + all subsequent rows – Repeat rows 2 and 3 to make the pattern until piece is roughly square.

Border – I just loved the range of yellows in this blanket, and I kept picturing a jet-black cat on it. So, I trimmed it with a single row of HDC, putting 3 HDC into each corner.

Key:

SS – Slip stitch
SC – Single crochet
YO – Yarn over
DC – Double crochet
CH – Chain
HDC – Half double crochet
TD – tear drop (YO, insert hook into CH 1 space and pull up a loop, YO and draw through 2 loops on hook. Do this three times, then YO and draw through all 4 loops on hook)

One of the secrets of life is that all that is really worth doing is what we do for others. ~ Lewis Carroll

What shelters have to say: "From all of us at Animal Care League, thank you so much for donating cozy blankets for our animals. All of the animals love them – especially the cats and kittens. We truly appreciate your on-going support to help our shelter animals feel as comfortable as possible while they wait to find forever homes. Thanks again!" ~ Animal Care League in Oak Park, IL

Very Comfy Blanket

This pattern combines flat areas, with rows of "V" stitches that really stand out. I think it adds a nice pattern and texture to the blanket. It also makes it very soft and comfy. I just love when the stitches create little puffs because to me it looks so comfy. I hope you agree!

You can use a single color, or variety, as I did. Each block of color did not require very much yarn, so this pattern would also be a great way to use up bits and pieces of leftover yarn. Every bit we keep out of the landfills is a win!

Gather your comfort tools - I suggest using 4-ply yarn and a "K" sized hook.

Get started helping pets - CH 50.

Row 1 – SC in second CH from hook and in each CH across to the end. CH1, turn.

Row 2 – SC in first 2 stitches, * TC in next stitch, SC in next 3 stitches, repeat from * across to the end, except put a SC into each of the last 4 stitches, CH 1, turn.

Row 3 – SC in each stitch across, CH 1, turn.

Row 4 – SC in first stitch, * TC **AROUND BAR** of next TC that is 2 rows below. (*You'll want to approach the stitch from the right, when you're going around the bar. This creates a RTC stitch!*) To continue, skip the next stitch, SC in next stitch, RTC **AROUND**

BAR of <u>the same TC</u> you already used for the previous RTC, being sure to go under the previous RTC. *(This time you'll be approaching from the left.)* To continue, skip the next stitch, SC in next stitch, repeat from * across to end. CH 1, turn.

- *Note: Make sure you're going around the TC that is 2 rows down from where you're working. I found this, at first, to be a bit awkward to do. If you stick with it, it gets easier! Also, be sure to put the second RTC under the first RTC that you are putting around the TC.*

Row 5 – Repeat row 3.

Rows 6 to 9 – Repeat rows 2 – 5.

Row 10 + 11 – Start new color and complete 2 rows of DC, across to the end.

Row 12+ - (I changed to a new yarn color). Repeat rows 2 – 11, five times. This creates a nice size blanket that is roughly 20" wide and 22" long.

Border – As always, lots of different borders will work for this blanket. There's enough going on already, that a fancy border is not needed. For the sample, I put a row of SC to match the color I used for the DC rows (white), with 3 SC in each corner. I then found a fun variegated yarn and added a row of HDC (3 in each corner) to tie all the colors together!

Key:
CH – chain
DC – double crochet
TC - triple crochet
RTC – raised triple crochet
SC – single crochet

What shelters have to say: "*Thank you so much for the handmade blankets you sent to our shelter, for our cats and dogs. They absolutely love them! They love to snuggle on them and keep warm on these especially chilly days. Your kindness means so much to us. Thanks for caring for our homeless "kids".*
~ Hillside SPCA in Pottsville, PA

Fangs for Fun

I found that creating these little "fangs" was fun and super easy! I also appreciated learning this technique, since it can be mixed into any pattern, which you may already have, to create something truly special! You can add lots of "fangs" or just put a few here and there. The sample I created is somewhere in between! I used three colors of yarn for the sample, but at least two colors are required so that you can clearly see the fangs. It's a fun pattern, I hope you'll give it a try!

Gather your comfort tools - I suggest using 4-ply yarn and a "K" sized hook for best results. I do think thick yarn would work fine and even doubling up and using two strands would work.

Get started helping pets - CH 48.

Row 1 – SC in second CH from the hook and in each CH across to the end. Change to a new color yarn. CH1, turn.

Row 2 – SC in the first 2 stitches, * SC at **BASE** (not the top of the stitch, as usual) of next stitch (this creates the "fang"), SC in next 2 stitches, repeat from * across to the end (except put a SC into the last 3 stitches), CH 1, turn.

Row 3 – CH 2, DC in each stitch across.

Row 4 – CH 1, turn, SC in each stitch across to the end. Change to new color yarn.

Row 5+ - Repeat rows 2 to 4 until you reach the size blanket you want. You'll be changing yarn color every time you start a new repeat.

Border – For the border, I went back to the first color I used, and added a row of SC around the other 3 sides. I then continued, putting a couple rows of HDC all around the perimeter. As always, be sure to put 3 stitches into each corner of any border stitch you use.

Key: CH – chain
DC – double crochet
SC – single crochet
HDC - half double crochet

Service to others is the rent you pay for your room here on earth. ~ Muhammad Ali

Why volunteers help: "I know how grim animal shelters can be. I've volunteered and worked for pay at several shelters, and all too often, cats and dogs only have newspaper to lie on. Blankets make such a positive difference in their lives. And when they're happy, they get noticed more, and they get adopted!" *~ Hazel B-M in Tallahassee, FL*

Criss-Cross Crochet

This pattern was suggested by Michael A. of Boston, MA and I loved it as soon as I tried it. It involves working behind stitches to make an "X" shape (see picture at right) and creates thick and fluffy blankets. I did find that I had to watch what I was doing (usually I don't), and not be glued to watching the TV. That's not necessarily a bad thing! If you try it, the stitch will get a lot easier as you go and it's just perfect for pet blankets. Thank you Michael!

Gather your comfort tools – I suggest using 4-ply yarn and a "K" sized hook for best results, but thicker yarn and a larger hook would work too.

Get started helping pets - CH about 50, depending on the thickness of the yarn and your stitch gauge. Chain should measure approximately 18-20" from start to hook.

Row 1 – SC in second CH from hook and in each chain across to the end.

Row 2 – CH 2, turn, *skip the next chain and work a DC in the next chain, then working behind the DC you just made, work a DC in the chain you deliberately skipped (CC made!). Repeat from * all the way to the end, putting a DC into the last ST.

Row 3 – CH 2, turn, HDC into top of each ST across to the end.

Row 4+ – Alternate row 2 and 3 until the pet blanket is somewhat square.

Final Row – Your final row should be SC all the way across, rather than doing row 3 (HDC across).

Border – Any type of border can be applied to this piece, from a simple SC to something more elaborate. To duplicate the blanket pictured, add two rows of HDC in each ST along the perimeter, putting three HDCs into each corner.

Key:

CH – chain

DC – double crochet

HDC - half double crochet

SC – single crochet

CC – crossed crochet (skip next chain & work DC in the next chain, then working behind the DC you just made, work a DC in the chain you deliberately skipped!)

Why volunteers help: "My 2 pet dogs and cat are my best friends – all have been adopted. Throughout my life dogs and cats have been part of my family and they are very special to me. I think the blankets will keep them warm and secure and hopefully they will feel the love being sent with each and every blanket I made." ~ *Irene M. in Huntington, NY*

The people who make the biggest difference in the world, are the people who make small ones each and every day. ~ Robert Clancy

Basically Beautiful Blanket

This is one of the easiest patterns in this book, especially for beginners. It's also a good way to learn the foundation stitches (at least in my opinion) of crochet. It's comprised of single crochet, half-double crochet and double-crochet stitches. If you find you get bored with patterns that have you doing the same stitch, row after row, you'll like this one that changes things up. Enjoy!

Gather your comfort tools - I suggest using two strands of 4-ply yarn and a "N" size hook. With this combo the blanket works up fast and is nice and thick. The end result is about 18"x 20" which is a great size.

Get started comforting pets - CH 31.

Row 1 – SC in second chain from hook, and across to the end.

Row 2 – CH2, turn, HDC in 2nd chain from hook and across to the end.

Row 3 – CH2, turn, DC in 2nd chain from hook and across to the end.

Row 4 – Repeat row 2.

Row 5 – Repeat row 1. *After this row I changed yarn color...so feel free to do so, if you want!*

Row 6 - 10 – Repeat pattern formed by rows 1 to 5. In total, you'll repeat the pattern five times to form 6 stripes.

Border – Any type of border can be applied to this piece. For the sample, I did a SC all the way around, putting three SCs into each corner. I then added a second border of HDC, all around, with three HDCs in each corner.

Key:

CH – chain

SC – single crochet

DC – double crochet

HDC - half double crochet

> *What shelters have to say:* "Thank you so much for the wonderful blankets we received at our shelter. The cats just love them and it feels so much more like a home until they find theirs! We appreciate you!" ~ *Wabash County Shelter in Mt. Carmel, IL*

Victory for Pets

This is a really cute stitch to make. As with all the patterns I seem to enjoy, it was easy to do and went fast. The holes are not terribly large, so shelters will use the blanket for all sorts of pets. I can just see a puppy cuddling this blanket!

Gather your comfort tools - I suggest using 4-ply yarn and a "K" sized hook for best results.

Get started helping pets – CH 44 loosely (and I do mean loosely). I had to re-start a couple times to make it loose enough, so learn from my mishaps!

Row 1 - DC, CH 1, DC all in fifth chain from hook (V-Stitch made). *Skip next two CHs, work VS in next CH. Repeat from * all the way across to the last 2 CHs, DC in last CH.

Row 2 – CH 3, turn, work VS in each "Chain 1 spaces" across, DC in top of beginning CH.

Repeat - Repeat row 2 until piece measures 18 – 20 inches.

Border – I created a simple border with three rows of HDC (putting 3 HDC into each corner). I had just a bit of extra yarn, which I used for the first and third rows, and made the second row from the same yarn I used for the blanket. Whatever you decide, have fun!

<u>Key:</u>
CH – Chain

DC – Double crochet
SC – Single crochet
HDC – Half double crochet
VS – Victory Stitch (2 DC, CH1, 2 DC all in same stitch)

Why volunteers help: *"I want to give them some kind of comfort while waiting for their forever home. I am disabled, and not working, so this not only helps them, but me. A win-win situation as they say since I cannot physically or financially help. I hope the blankets will bring them comfort, warmth, and hopefully desensitize the environment for them. Also, it will absorb sound and make it, I am hoping, a little less overwhelming and stressful."* **~ Ina S. in Mountain Home, ID**

Waffles Anyone?

If you're interested in making a mini-mattress to comfort a shelter pet, this is the pattern for you! I was a bit hesitant at first (it looked difficult and I love to mindlessly crochet)….but I ended up loving the stitch. Be sure to give it at least a few rows, so that you can see the design take shape. I almost gave up too early, but I'm glad I didn't.

Gather your comfort tools - I suggest using 4-ply yarn and an "I" sized hook for best results.

Get started helping pets - CH 52.

Row 1 – DC in the third CH from the hook and in each CH across to the end.

Row 2 – CH 2, turn and begin work in the very first ST. *FPDC around the post in the next ST, DC in each of the next 2 ST, repeat from * to the end of the row.

Row 3 – CH 2, turn, DC in the first 2 ST, FPDC around the post of the next 2 ST, * DC in the next ST, FPDC in each of the next 2 ST, repeat from * until there's just 3 ST remaining. DC in next ST, FPDC in next ST, DC in final ST. *(In general, for this row you are putting a DC into the DCs in the previous row and a FPDC into the stitches that are "sticking out".)*

Row 4+ – Repeat rows 3 and 4 until you reach your desired size. *(For this row you are putting two FPDC into the two stitches that are pushing outward and a DC into the regular DC stitch in the previous row.)*

Final row – The final row for this blanket should be row #3, so that the "waffle squares" are all formed.

Border – For this stitch, I immediately started my border, with the same color I used for the blanket. I did this to "square" my blanket a bit and make it look more finished. I put a SC in each ST, then 3 SC into each corner, all the way around. Then I added a row of DC in a contrasting color, 2 rows of HDC, and a final row of DC. However, do feel free to be creative and use up whatever yarn you have!

Key:

CH – chain

DC – double crochet

ST – stitch

HDC – half double crochet

FPDC – front post double crochet (YO, insert hook all the way around the POST of next ST, going from FRONT to BACK, YO, pull up a loop, YO, draw through 2 loops, YO, draw through remaining 2 loops).

BPDC – back post double crochet (YO, insert hook all the way around the POST of next ST, going from BACK to FRONT, YO, pull up a loop, YO, draw through 2 loops, YO, draw through remaining 2 loops).

What shelters have to say: "What a lovely box of hand knit blankets we received for our animals! We really appreciate folks like you who are generous with their hands and hearts! Thank you so much for this generous gift." ~ Homeward Pet Adoption Center Shelter in Woodinville, WA

Cobblestones of Comfort

I LOVED doing this stitch, since the blanket that results is so thick (with just one strand of yarn)! It's really more like a soft, bumpy mattress. I couldn't help but envision a shelter pet snuggling into it. I think you're going to love the result as well. I also found it fun to create since it's versatile. As you add the "little bumps" in this pattern you can line them up or stagger them. Whatever you do … be creative and have fun!

Gather your comfort tools - I suggest using 4-ply yarn and a "K" sized hook for best results.

Get started helping pets - CH 52.

Row 1 – HDC in second CH from the hook and in each CH across to the end.

Row 2 – CH 1, turn, SC in first stitch, * TC in next stitch, SC in next stitch, repeat from * to the end of the row. *For this row, you'll either line up the "bumps" or stagger them. So just put the number of SC you need at the start to either line them up, or stagger them! For the pictured example I chose to stagger them.*

Row 3 – CH 2, turn, HDC in each stitch across to end.

Row 4+ – Repeat rows 2 and 3 until piece is roughly square, or whatever size you'd like.

Border – For this pattern it seemed important to add a border, to finish off the somewhat jagged edges. I added a row of SC all around the perimeter, with 3 SC in each corner. Since I loved the variegated yarn I found so much, I added another row of HDC all around (again with 3 HDC in each corner).

Key:

CH – chain

HDC - half double crochet

SC – single crochet

TC – triple crochet

What shelters have to say: "*We want to be sure you know how very, very much we appreciate the beautiful handmade blankets that have been provided for APL's animals. Staff members are excited when the blankets arrive, the animals find comfort, and the adopters are thrilled with them. Our gratitude to you and participants!*" *~ Animal Protective League in Springfield, IL*

Color Shift Clusters

  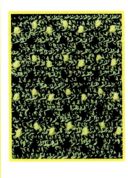

I did some experimentation with this pattern, seeing if I could switch between colors, mid-stream. Once you get started, you'll see what I mean! I enjoyed being creative, and hope you feel open to exploring your own creativity as you make blankets. There are no mistakes when it comes to pet blankets!

Gather your comfort tools - Crochet hook size N and 2 skeins of 4-ply yarn. This pattern is designed to use two strands of yarn worked together to make a soft and thick blanket!

Clusters:

- *For this pattern you'll be working a "cluster" stitch. To work a cluster: (YO, insert hook, pull up loop) 4X in same stitch, YO, pull loop through all loops on hook.*

- *I also wanted the clusters to be a solid color, even though I was using two strands. To make a color-shift cluster, I dropped one strand of yarn towards the front (black yarn for instance), and worked the cluster using only the yellow yarn, making sure I placed the hook under the loose black yarn, so that it was threaded through the center of the stitch. Once the cluster was done, I just picked up the black yarn and continued using two strands. After a couple rows of all yellow clusters, I switched and dropped the yellow yarn, resulting in some black clusters!*

- ***Special note:*** *This pattern has the "clusters" spaced 6 stitches apart. However, you can use any combination of clusters and HDCs that you like, even putting the clusters randomly throughout the blanket!*

Get started helping pets - CH 42

Row 1 – 1 HDC in 3rd CH from hook, and in each CH across. The result should be 41 stitches across.

Row 2 – CH2, HDC in nest 5 stitches, * CL in next stitch, HDC in each of next 6 stitches, repeat from *, ending with 6 HDCs.

Row 3 – CH2, HDC in each of next 8 stitches, * CL in next stitch, HDC in next 6 stitches, repeat from * across to end of row (however, the final group of HDCs will number 10).

Row 4 – CH2, HDC in each stitch across to the end.

Repeat – Repeat rows 2 – 4 until piece is square (or you run out of yarn!). I ended up with 25 rows, but it will depend on how tight or loose you crochet!

Border – Any type of border can be applied to this piece. I combined rows of SC and HDC, putting 3 stitches into every corner to square it off!

Key:

CH – Chain
CL – Cluster
HDC – Half Double Crochet
ST – Stitch
YO – Yarn over
SC – Single crochet

Some people don't understand why I help animals in need. I don't under stand why they wonder!

Why volunteers help: "I'm unable to leave the house to volunteer as I take care of my elderly mom. This gives me an opportunity to do good while still home bound. Also, it helps to minimize my mom's extreme stash of yarn!!" ~ *Barbara M. in Wheaton, IL*

Wandering Puffs

I really had fun with this pattern, since it was easy to do and it can be approached in a variety of ways. The main pattern I created has "puffs" showing up on either side of the blanket. Often shelters will flip over the blankets (in the case of dirt, etc.) so I wanted the blanket to look lovely both ways.

I've also included "alternate ways to use this stitch" after the pattern. One technique will put all the puffs on one side, and one which does not include the DC rows. Enjoy!

Gather your comfort tools - I suggest using 4-ply yarn and a "K" sized hook for best results. The yarn can be a bit thicker, but you may run into trouble managing the puffs, if the yarn is too thick.

Get started helping pets - CH 48, loosely.

Row 1 – SC in second CH from hook and in each CH across to the end.

Row 2 – CH 1, turn, SC in first 2 SC, * work a PUFF in next SC, SC in next 3 SC, repeat from * to end, putting 3 SC in last 3 SC of row.

Row 3 – CH 1, turn, SC in each SC across to end.

Row 4 – CH 1, turn, SC in first 4 SC, PUFF, * SC in next 3 SC, PUFF, repeat from * to end, putting SC in last 4 SC in row.

Row 5 – Repeat row 3.

Row 6 – Repeat row 2.

Row 7 – Repeat row 3.

Row 8 – Repeat row 4.

Row 9 – Repeat row 3.

Row 10 & 11 *(Done in a contrasting color)* – CH 2, turn, DC in each SC across to the end.

Repeat rows 1 to 11, until the blanket is square. Note: When you repeat row 1, just do CH1 and then SC across to the end. You'll likely need to do four sets of rows 1- 11. For the first and third sets the puffs will appear on the front. For the second and fourth sets the puffs will appear on the back. Note: For the fourth set, only do rows 1 – 9, making the final row of SC all the way across.

Border – Any type of border can be applied to this piece, from a simple SC to something more elaborate. To duplicate the blanket pictured, simply HDC in each stitch along the perimeter, putting three HDCs in each corner.

Alternate ways to use this stitch:

- You can also create a beautiful blanket, by simply doing the initial chain, row 1, and then alternate rows 2 and 3, until the blanket is the size you want.
- If you'd like a version of the blanket that has puffs on both sides, just do the initial chain, row 1 and then row 2 repeatedly, until it's the desired size.

Key:

YO – Yarn over
CH – Chain
DC – Double crochet
ST - Stitch
SC – Single crochet
PUFF – Puff stitch. Directions: YO and pull up a loop, 3 times in the same stitch, YO and draw through all 7 loops on hook.

Be part of something bigger than yourself.

Puffy V's

The first time I started a blanket with this pattern I used just one strand of yarn. After a few rows I really felt like it was too thin and lightweight for a warm, snuggly blanket. So I tried two strands and it made all the difference. Using two strands also allowed me to use leftover yarn (I didn't quite have a full skein of either color) and blend colors. I would recommend this technique, unless there's a really thick yarn you enjoy using! The pattern worked up a blanket quickly and I liked the result. I hope you have fun with this pattern too!

Gather your comfort tools - Use crochet hook size N and two colors of 4-ply yarn (to make a blanket as it appears in the pictures). You'll see that for some rows I used two strands of the same color, and then used one strand of each color for other rows. Just be creative and use up the yarn you have. This blanket is just perfect for that approach!

Get started helping pets - CH 42.

Row 1 – DC in fourth CH from hook and in each chain across to the end.

Row 2 – CH 1, turn, SC in first DC, CH 2, skip next DC, SC in space before next DC, CH 2,* skip next 2 DC, SC in space before next DC, CH2, repeat from * across to last 2 ST, and put SC into the top of the beginning CH.

Row 3 – CH 3, turn, DC in next ST, 2 DC in each CH-2 space across to the last CH-2 space, then put DC into last SC and DC into the top of the CH.

Row 4 – 32 – Repeat rows 2 and 3 until you reach the desired size. Change colors, whenever you run out of yarn or whenever you want to. Be creative! I needed to do 32 rows, but you may end up doing a few more or a few less.

Border – Any type of border can be applied to this piece, from a simple SC to something more elaborate. For my blanket I kept it simple and just put two rows of HDC all around the perimeter (putting 3 HDC into each corner).

Key:
CH – chain
DC - double crochet
SC – single crochet
ST – stitch
HDC – half double crochet

I stitch a piece of my heart into everything I crochet!

Why volunteers help: "I made blankets because I wanted to help the kitties feel loved and comforted. I think you're doing God's work in a tangible way and helping anyone who wants to help become involved. Bless you!"
~ Jo R. in Western Springs, IL

Super-Comfy Spikes?

This "spike" stitch may not sound comfy at all, but I assure you it is! I really enjoy learning new stitches, so that I can be creative with the blankets I make and add a bit of "spice" when I want to! You'll find that for many "basic" patterns, you can just add a row of spikes that will stand out, especially if you change colors! This stitch also adds quite a bit of thickness to a blanket, even when only one strand of yarn is used. Enjoy!

Gather your comfort tools - I suggest using 4-ply yarn and a "K" sized hook for best results, but thicker yarn and a larger hook would work too.

Get started helping pets – CH45 loosely.

Row 1 – SC in second CH from hook and in each CH across.

Row 2 – CH1, turn, SC in each SC across to end.

Row 3 – CH1, turn, SC in first SC, * SPIKE stitch, SC, repeat from * across to end, except put 2 SCs in last 2 SC. *You're simply doing one SC and then one SPIKE all the way across.*

Row 4 – CH1, turn, * SPIKE, SC, repeat from * across to end.

Row 5+ - Repeat rows 3 and 4, until you reach the finished size you want. *You're basically alternating between starting a row with SC, and starting the next row with a SPIKE. Then as you crochet the rows, you're putting a SPIKE into any SC, and putting a SC into any SPIKE!*

Final Rows – I did the final two rows as SCs across to the end, to match the beginning of the blanket and gives it a nice, finished look. I changed colors every 8 rows, which was about 3". This created a blanket with a finished size of 20" x 20".

Border – Any type of border can be applied to this piece. For the sample (pictured) I chose a simple SC all around the perimeter, putting three SCs in each corner.

Key:

CH – chain

SC – single crochet

YO – yarn over

SPIKE – Spike stitch. Directions: Insert hook in SC **BELOW** the next SC (this is the same stitch that the next SC was worked), pull up loop even with your hook, YO and draw through both hoops on the hook. *You're doing a basic SC, except you're going into the stitch below where you normally would!*

Never get tired of doing little things for others. Sometimes those little things occupy the biggest part of their hearts.

What shelters have to say: "Thank you so much. These beds are fantastic. So cozy and such beautiful colors. Our kitties, young and old, will truly appreciate these wonderful gifts!" ~ Feline Friends in Olympia, WA

Here Fishy Fishy

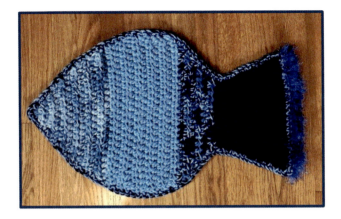

Whatever you do, have fun with this pattern! Create a long fish, wide fish, large fish or small fish. The great thing about making blankets for pets, is that they are not at all picky. Experiment and create a wacky fish, if you want! I found that the final touch of adding a border all around, really makes it all comes together. I used a bit of eyelash yarn on the tail, just for accent, but it's not completely necessary. I enjoyed creating my large fish blankets so much that I even gave away a few to friends!

Gather your comfort tools - I suggest using two strands of 4-ply yarn and a "K" size hook. With this combo the blanket works up fast and is nice and thick. The finished blanket is roughly 16"x 26", and ideal for kitties that like to "lounge".

Get started helping pets - Row 1: CH 2, 2 HDC in 2nd ch from hook. CH 1 and turn.

Row 2: 2 HDC in 1st ST, 2 HDC in last ST. CH 1 and turn.

Row 3: 2 HDC in 1st ST, HDC in next 2 ST, 2 HDC in last ST. CH 1 and turn.

Row 4: 2 HDC in 1st ST, HDC in next 4 ST, 2 HDC in last ST. CH 1 and turn.

Row 5: 2 HDC in 1st ST, HDC in next 6 ST, 2 HDC in last ST. CH 1 and turn.

Row 6: 2 HDC in 1st ST, HDC in next 8 ST, 2 HDC in last ST. CH 1 and turn.

Row 7: 2 HC in 1st ST, HDC in next 10 ST, 2 HDC in last ST. CH 1 and turn.

Row 8: 2 HDC in 1st ST, HDC in next 12 ST, 2 HDC in last ST. CH 1 and turn.

Row 9 - 20: Do 6 <u>sets</u> of rows that alternate between first doing an expanding row (with 2 HDC at beginning & end) and a row of HDC across.

Row 21 - 24: Do 4 rows of HDC across.

Row 25 - 30: Do 6 rows that alternate contracting rows (combine 2 HDC* together at beginning & end) & rows of HDC.

Row 31 - 44: Do 5 <u>sets</u> of rows that alternate expanding rows (2 HDC at beginning & end) & rows of HDC.

Border: Trim entire fish in HDC all around.

Fish tail: Add 2 rows of SC eyelash (or similar) yarn to end of tail. Make it as fluffy as you like, by adding more rows!

<u>**Key:**</u>
CH – chain
ST – stitch
HDC - half double crochet
SC – single crochet
2 HDC together - *YO, insert hook into next stitch, YO and pull up a loop, do this two times, then another YO and pull through all 5 loops.*

A kind gesture can reach a wound that only compassion can heal. - Steve Maraboli

What shelters have to say: "Thank you for the beautiful blankets and the bonus scratching disc. During kitten season the blankets go fast. You have wonderful, talented volunteers. Did you ever think your efforts would have grown into what it has? So many animals have you and your volunteers to thank for a warm, snuggly blanket to comfort them while they wait for their forever homes." ~ *Animal Rescue Foundation in Lisle, IL*

Rainbow Promise

This pattern blends the cuteness of fleece with the softness and bright colors of vibrant yarn. The rainbow of colors around the perimeter represent the promise we make to the pets we adopt. We'll be there for them, good or bad, much like the promise God made to mankind, with the rainbow. So, this is one of my very favorite blankets to make for pets!

Gather your comfort tools - You'll need two crochet hooks, size K and N. You'll also need two 14" wide pieces of fleece, an awl (or rotary cutter) to poke holes around the perimeter, and yarn in the colors of purple, blue, green, yellow, orange and red. Of course, you can use yarn in any color combination, but I really like to duplicate the colors of the rainbow. I doubled the yarn, and used two strands together, just to make the blanket thicker.

Get started helping pets:

Prep the fleece – Place two pieces of fleece together with the more vibrant sides facing outward. Cut both pieces together, to a perimeter of approximately 14". I used a safety pin to hold them together, since you don't want them to shift at all. I found if they shifted it was hard to line them up perfectly again!

Next, use an awl or rotary cutter with the appropriate blade to cut holes approximately ¼" apart along the perimeter of both pieces of fleece. I kept the pieces pinned and just lifted the top piece a bit to use my rotary cutter. I placed the holes about ½" from the edge. These holes form the foundation you'll be using as you crochet around the perimeter.

Row 1 in black *(two strands used for all the colors)* – Use crochet hook size K and SC into each hole along the perimeter, tie off and weave in ends.

Row 2 in purple – Switch to crochet hook N (which you'll use for the rest of the blanket). Join new color into any SC stitch. HDC into each SC all around the perimeter, tie off and weave in ends.

Row 3 in blue – Join new color into any HDC stitch. HDC into each stitch all around the perimeter, tie off and weave in ends.

Row 4 in green – Join new color into any HDC stitch. HDC into each stitch all around the perimeter, tie off and weave in ends.

Row 5 in yellow – Join new color into any HDC stitch. For this row, you'll still put HDCs all around the perimeter, but you'll enlarge the row a bit by putting 2 HDCs into every 16th HDC. Then tie off and weave in ends.

Row 6 in orange – Join new color into any HDC stitch. HDC into each HDC all around the perimeter, putting two HDCs every time you run into a double-HDC stitch.

Row 7 in red – Join new color into any HDC stitch. HDC into each HDC all around the perimeter, putting two HDCs every time you run into a double-HDC stitch.

Final Row in black – Your final row should be SC all around the perimeter, tie off and weave in ends.

Key:
HDC - half double crochet
SC – single crochet

Why volunteers help: "I have three Pugapoos and love animals. Since my husband won't let me get any more dogs, this is my way of loving them from afar! I hope the blankets give the cats and dogs comfort and a feeling of home!" ~ Jennifer T. in Acton, ME

CFC Temperature Blanket

This is a super-easy blanket that you can do with whatever crochet stitch you'd like or hook size. It's a fun way to look back and see how cold, hot, or varied the weather was during the month. Here are some basic directions, based on how I created mine. It should result in a blanket that's approximately 20"x20" (but as always, anything remotely close is fine!). *Feel free to be creative!*

Gather your comfort tools – You'll need a hook size: K (6.5mm) and 4-ply washable yarn in the appropriate colors (see thermometer) for your current season.

Get started helping pet - Chain 50, turn, complete a HDC in the second chain from hook and in every chain across to the end.

- Create one row each day, which reflects the temperature outside (according to the thermometer). I used different shades of the colors as I went, just to make it more colorful.
- At the end of each row, make your final HDC into the top of the stitch, and you're done for the day. Each day you'll then attach a new color (if needed), chain 2 and turn to complete the row for the day!

>90 = RED

75-89 = ORANGE

60-74 = YELLOW

45-59 = GREEN

32-44 = BLUE

< 32 = PURPLE

< 10 = BLACK!

Key:
HDC - half double crochet

My "January" temperature blanket!

Mini-Hearts for Blankets

Sometimes a blanket is finished, but it seems to need just a little bit more. Since "love" for the homeless pets was woven into every stitch, adding one of these little hearts is the perfect finishing touch. They are also fun and quick to create! Give it a whirl and you may be making them for all your pet blankets!

Gather your comfort tools:
- Small amount of yarn to match the blanket which will receive the heart. Be sure to pick a color that will easily blend in, when you attach it using the "tails" of the finished heart.
- Crochet hook in the size range of I, J or K. For the photographs above, I used hook size I to create the red heart, J for the dark pink heart and K for the light pink heart.

Get started helping pets:
This heart is made by working a series of different length stitches all into the first chain. It's so easy!

- CH 4, then work 3 TC into first chain (chain farthest from the hook).
- While still working in the first CH, work 3 DC, CH 1, 1 TC, CH 1, 3 DC, 3 TC, CH 3.

- The next step really defines the "heart" shape. Join with SS to same "first chain" at the center that you've been working into.
- Pull the yarn tail from the beginning stitch to tighten and define the heart. Cut the yarn and fasten off, leaving a 3-4 inch piece. Use both "tails", from the beginning and the end of the piece, to attach the heart to your blanket.

Key:

CH = Chain

DC = Double crochet

TC = Triple crochet

SS = Slip stitch

Why volunteers help: "I care a lot about animals, and I wanted to help by giving them something to help them feel comfortable. Since I can't adopt all of the homeless animals, this is an effective and efficient way to help." ~Anushka N. in Wildwood, MO

Add Puffs to Your Blankets

Some CFC volunteers make astounding blankets which have "puff patterns" in them (see sample at right, not made by me!). They use a solid color yarn and then add 3D outlines of cats, hearts, paw prints and more.

Adding an outline of virtually any simple shape to your blanket takes just four steps:

- Sketch an outline of the image you want to add.
- Learn the Puff stitch (directions on the next page).
- As you create the rows in your blanket, simply replace the typical stitch you would use with one Puff stitch. In the sample below I created rows of half-double crochet and then substituted the puff stitch wherever I wanted the image outline to fall. I started with a simple heart, so I was able to visually tell where the replacement-Puff should be.
- Have fun...and yes, that's a step. You may need to pull out a row and do it over a few times (or maybe it's just me), but isn't that the fun of creating something anyway? So try wacky designs and never stop trying new things!

Puff Stitch

Instead of the stitch you would normally do next in the row, take these steps to create a "puff":

- ✓ 5 DC in the same space
- ✓ Drop the loop from the hook
- ✓ Insert hook in first DC of 5-DC group
- ✓ Hook dropped loop and draw through
- ✓ CH 1 to close

Key:

DC – Double crochet

CH – Chain

No act of kindness, no matter how small, is ever wasted. ~Aesop

What shelters have to say: "Thank you so much for the beautiful blankets you send on a regular basis. Our animals are more comfortable and happier with your blankets, and we are grateful for your kindness and thoughtfulness. What you do for animals and shelters is amazing!" ~Upper Valley Humane Society in Enfield, NH

Edging:
The Finishing Touch!

One of the many things I appreciate about our blankets is that they really show off the love and caring we have for homeless pets. Crafters tend to forget that not everyone is a "fiber artist", and so when an adoptive family meets a dog or cat, wrapped in a beautiful hand-crafted blanket, they are impressed! They are even more thrilled to find out their new family member gets to take it home!

A great finishing touch to a blanket is a decorative trim. It's a wonderful way to add color, cover some uneven side-stitches or make a small blanket a bit bigger. Here are four ideas for the perfect trim to add to any crocheted blanket. Try one of these, or just do a simple half-double crochet around the perimeter. The only "trick" is to make sure you put three stitches into every corner!

CRAB STITCH

The Crab Stitch makes a wonderful edging and is quite easy to complete. It's clean, simple design nicely frames a blanket.

Work one row of SC in the edging yarn, around the blanket, putting three stitches into each corner. When you get to the end, do not turn. CH 1, skip the stitch directly to the RIGHT, and *reverse single crochet* (R-SC*) into each SC, ending with a SS into the beginning chain.

*R-SC (worked from left to right): Insert hook in next stitch to the right, yarn over, pull loop through, yarn over, pull through both loops on hook.

SHELLS

This edging is a bit fancy, but not much work. It's the perfect touch for many blanket styles.

It may be easier to work a row of SC along the perimeter of the blanket first. Be sure to put three SC into each corner. Then CH 1, SC in first ST, *skip 1 ST, 5 DC in next ST, skip 1 ST, 1 SC in next ST. Repeat from * to end, SC into last ST.

PICOTS

This is another great edging to add a bit of elegance to any blanket. Try using a surprising color, which will really be a contrast to the rest of the blanket. Remember, when you're an artist, there are no mistakes!

For this edging you're doing SC as the trim and adding a "picot" as you go! Create your first SC and then CH 4 or 5 (depending how large you want the Picot) and SS into the first CH. Now you have a Picot! Next work 3 or 4 SC into the next 3 or 4 stitches (depending how far apart you want the Picots) and then make another Picot. Continue around the perimeter of the blanket.

T-EDGE

This edging also gives a very clean line to a blanket and really looks best in a highly-contrasting color. It uses a "Spike Single Crochet" (S-SC) that's simple to do!

CH 1, SC in first 3 ST, *1 S-SC in next stitch (make the spike by inserting your hook about 1/4" below the edge, or longer if you like!), 1 SC in each of the next 3 ST. Repeat from * to end.

<u>Key:</u>
CH = Chain
DC = Double crochet
R-SC = Reverse single crochet
SC = Single crochet
SS = Slip stitch
S-SC = Spike single crochet
ST = Stitch

Curly Qs

This pattern makes adorable toys, which kitties are just crazy for! It's a wonderful way to use up those little bits of yarn you may have left over, after making a blanket. I like to include a couple color-coordinated Curly Qs with every blanket I personally make and donate.

To make them even more special, I borrow an idea from Kathy W. at the Chenango SPCA. I make a handful of Curly Qs and then put them in a large zip-lock bag with some catnip for a couple days. Once I take them out and shake the catnip back into the bag for future use, they are off to a shelter with the blankets I ship. But beware … you may have to hide them from your own cats. I know I do!

Gather your comfort tools - I suggest using 4-ply yarn and a "H" sized hook.

Get started helping pets – CH30.

Create the curl – Put 2 SCs in 2nd CH from hook, then 3 SCs into each CH across to the end. Done! My Curly Q measured about 1 ¼" x 5"...a great size for kitties!

Key:

CH – chain

SC – single crochet

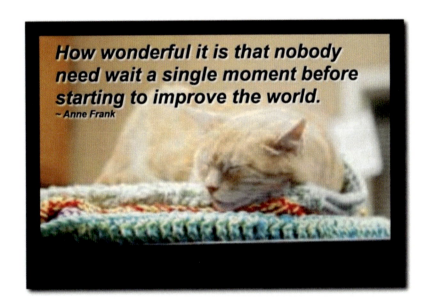

BLANKET TIPS

I sincerely hope you enjoyed making those blankets! I loved creating the patterns, testing out colors and trying to come up with the 30 "perfect patterns for pets!" I'd like to leave you with a few comments about making blankets. Some of these sentiments have already been mentioned, but they certainly deserve repeating!

First and foremost, I always encourage a new volunteer to follow their heart and create whatever they feel called to work on. Sometimes it's large dog blankets, other times it's crocheted toys. Rest assured that everything always finds a home! Please keep this in mind as you craft your blankets using the patterns I've provided. There are no "wrong" blankets!

With that said, there are a few guidelines to keep in mind…

The more color the better!

Shelters love to be bright and cheery, and our colorful blankets can really help. Don't be afraid to use super-bright colors and combine colors in unusual ways. The more color the better, which even includes adding a bright trim on a blanket, or including a colorful "Curly Q" toy.

Also keep in mind that a completely white, or black, blanket tends to show every bit of dirt. It's fine to mix in black or white yarn, but do try to blend it with something colorful!

Washable is a must!

The only real requirement for our blankets is that they are washable and machine-dryable. The shelters launder the blankets on a regular basis, so they need to stand up to lots of washing and drying (and cuddling and kneading!).

No worries!

Do NOT worry if the blanket isn't the perfect size, shape or perfectly done! Even though we provide some general suggestions on size, the shelters will use whatever you create. They help all sorts of pets, in all sorts of sizes, so whatever you make will be used by the shelter and loved by their pets.

No strings attached!

I hate weaving in the ends as much as the next crafter, but it is an important step for pet blankets. Volunteers sometimes ask if they can leave loose ends for the pets to play with. This is a sweet thought, but a loose string could also be ingested. So be sure to weave in all ends, as the final step in making a blanket. I use a blunt tapestry needle to do my weaving and it's really not as bad as you think!

Forget the fancy yarn!

The many gorgeous yarns on the market can be quite tempting! Please remember though that it has to be washable, and quite durable, since it will be used and loved a lot! The fancy yarns are sometimes washable, but they usually need to "dry flat" which isn't possible in a shelter setting. These yarns are also expensive, so save some money and treat yourself to twice the number of skeins of "basic" washable 4ply yarn.

Tags anyone?

I've seen some wonderful, thoughtful tags added to individual blankets that I receive for distribution to shelters. These are just awesome! I'd suggest though that a larger tag, placed on top of a group of blankets may be enough. Remember that these blankets are not put on a shelf, but are put into an enclosure right away! So, the individual tags will be removed once the blanket is being used, which will be almost immediately. The same sentiments, put on a card at the top of the box or bag, will surely be appreciated by the shelter staff.

I'd also like you to think long-term, so that you can continue to help shelter pets in whatever way works for you. Sometimes people tire of making blankets after a while, and that's okay. There are many ways for you to help shelter pets, which don't require yarn. For any of these ideas, please contact your local shelter, for more information.

- **Transporting animals** from shelters in rural areas to those in more populous areas, which have higher adoption rates.
- **Foster an animal** in your home. Yes, it's a big commitment, but it might just warm your heart in ways you can't imagine!

- **Volunteer at a shelter!** Tasks range from the mundane (cleaning cages) to delightful (petting kittens), but they all need to be done. They will appreciate whatever you can do to help!

- **Donate items to shelters**, other than blankets. Most shelters have a "wish list" posted on their website, so this is a great place to start. They may also have a wish list created on Amazon. So, you can stay home, select some items, and they will be shipped (free if you use Prime) to the shelter!

- **Take photographs** of adoptable pets. This can be more time-consuming for the shelter than you would think, so it's a big help.

- Use your own **social media** channels to help spread the word on a shelter you choose. Promote their adoption events, share pictures of the pets in their care, or post their wish list for your family and friends to see.

- **Donate pet food** to your community food pantry. Most pantries will accept pet food, since they realize the important role of pets in their client's lives. Your contribution will help the pet, and the person who loves them.

- Make a **monetary donation**. In the end, all non-profits can always use more cash! There are vet bills to take care of, supplies to purchase, and sometimes staff to pay. All of which can be solved with funding. So, as your budget permits, consider making a donation. I can personally tell you that every bit helps, and every dollar is appreciated. If you can only afford a $5 donation, don't let that stop you from donating!

Although I provided quite a few ideas, a quick call to your local shelter is also a great way to start. They will know exactly what will help them out, and help out their pets, the best!

In the end, it's not about using up extra yarn, or filling time while we watch TV. It's about Anna, before she was adopted, and about her brother Benjamin who had to wait a bit longer for his forever family. Just as choosing between them was one of the hardest decisions I've ever made, starting up Comfort for Critters was one of the easiest. I knew the minute I felt that tap on my shoulder, what I was called to do and just how unprepared I was for the journey ahead. CFC grew up around me, and sometimes in spite of me, and I'm grateful to play my role. **A gigantic thank you goes to every single person, from 2007 to today, who has helped along the way.**

May God continue to bless you,
just as you have blessed others!

Connect Online

We'd love for you to keep up-to-date on what we're doing to comfort homeless pets. Please subscribe to our free newsletter or follow us on social media!

Critters News   www.comfortforcritters.org/newsletter-subscription

Comfort for Critters Website   www.ComfortForCritters.org

Email   Info@ComfortForCritters.org

Facebook   https://www.facebook.com/ComfortforCritters/

Feel free to also join the private, "The Comfort for Critters Team" Facebook group

Sources & Inspiration

1. The American Humane Association, www.americanhumane.org

2. The National Animal Care & Control Association, NACA, www.nacanet.org

3. The American Society for the Prevention of Cruelty to Animals, ASPCA, www.aspca.org

4. The Society of Animal Welfare Administrators, SAWA, www.sawanetwork.org

5. American Pet Products Association, APPA, www.americanpetproducts.org

6. People for the Ethical Treatment of Animals, PETA, www.peta.org

7. Shelter Animals Count, www.shelteranimalscount.org

8. National Council on Pet Population Study & Policy, NCPPSP, www.petpopulation.org

9. "What helps shelter dogs get adopted and stay in homes?", June 21, 2017, Zazie Todd, PhD

10. "Homing and re-homing Fido: How many newly-adopted pets are still kept six months later?", June 12, 2014, Zazie Todd, PhD

11. "Adoption and relinquishment interventions at the animal shelter", 2017, A. Protopopova & L.M. Gunter

12. Orvis News, January 2019, news.orvis.com/dogs/pet-adoption-statistics-the-numbers-behind-the-need

13. New York Times, September 3, 2019, www.nytimes.com/2019/09/03/upshot/why-euthanasia-rates-at-animal-shelters-have-plummeted.html

14. American Humane Association, 2013, Keeping pets in homes: A three-phase retention study. www.americanhumane.org/petsmart-keeping-pets-phase-ii.pdf

15. "5 Dog Nose Facts Your Probably Didn't Know", Aly Semigran, Petmd, www.petmd.com

16. "5 Senses: Cats vs. Humans", October 6, 2009, www.lovemeow.com

17. "Shelter Dogs Live Up to Expectations (Mostly)," January 27, 2016, Zazie Todd, PhD

18. "The History of Science in Animal Shelters", April 30,2016, Julie Hecht

19. "Animal Shelters", www.learningtogive.org

20. "The Science of Animal Shelters: An Inspirational Series", April 14, 2016, Julie Hecht

21. "25 Creative ways to help animal shelters", March 13, 2014, Jaymi Heimbuch

22. "Ten ways to help your local shelter or rescue", The Humane Society of the United States, www.humanesociety.org/resources/ten-ways-help-your-local-shelter-or-rescue

23. "8 Ways you can help shelter animals without adopting", Puppy Leaks, www.puppyleaks.com/help-shelter-animals-without-adopting/

24. Every single Comfort for Critters volunteer and supporter! They are a great information source and they inspire me, in our mission, every day!

Made in the USA
Monee, IL
17 December 2023